· · ·

H A N S   H O L Z E R

TALES AT MIDNIGHT

• • •

H A N S   H O L Z E R

TALES AT MIDNIGHT

TRUE STORIES FROM PARAPSYCHOLOGY
CASEBOOKS AND JOURNALS

COURAGE
BOOKS

an imprint of
RUNNING PRESS
Philadelphia, Pennsylvania

Canadian representatives: General Publishing Co., Ltd.,
30 Lesmill Road, Don Mills, Ontario M3B 2T6.

International representatives: Worldwide Media Services, Inc.,
30 Montgomery Street, Jersey City, New Jersey 07302.

9 8 7 6 5 4 3 2 1
Digit on the right indicates the number of this printing.

Library of Congress Catalog Card Number 93–085540
ISBN 1–56138–391–0

Cover illustration by Phillip Singer
Cover design by Toby Schmidt
Edited by Virginia Mattingly
Typography: Berkeley Oldstyle by Deborah Lugar

Published by Courage Books, an imprint of
Running Press Book Publishers
125 South Twenty-second Street
Philadelphia, Pennsylvania 19103–4399

CONTENTS

INTRODUCTION

What exactly is a ghost? Something people dream up in their cups or on a sickbed? Something you read about in juvenile fiction? Far from it. Ghosts—apparitions of "dead" people or sounds associated with invisible human beings—are the surviving emotional memories of people. They are people who have not been able to make the transition from their physical state into the world of the spirit—or as Dr. Joseph Rhine of Duke University has called it, the world of the *mind*. Their state is one of emotional shock induced by sudden death or great suffering, and because of it the individuals involved cannot understand what is happening to them. They are unable to see beyond their own immediate environment or problem, and so they are forced to continually relive those final moments of agony until someone breaks through and explains things to them. In this respect they are like psychotics being helped by the psychoanalyst, except that the patient is not on the couch, but rather in the atmosphere of destiny. Man's electromagnetic nature makes this perfectly plausible; that is, since our individual personality is really nothing more than a personal energy field encased in a denser outer layer called the physical body, the personality can store emotional stimuli and memories indefinitely without much dimming, very much like a tape recording that can be played over and over without losing clarity or volume.

Those who die normally under conditions of adjustment need not go through this agony, and they seem to pass on rapidly into that next state of consciousness that may be a "heaven" or a "hell," according to what the individual's mental state at death might have been. Neither state is an objective place, but is a subjective state of being. The sum total of similar states of being may, however, create a quasi-objective state approaching a condition or "place" along more orthodox religious lines. My contact with the confused individuals unable to depart from the earth's sphere, those who are commonly called "ghosts," is through a trance medium who will lend her physical body temporarily to the entities so that they can speak through her and detail their problems, frustrations, or unfinished business. Here again, the parallel with psychoanalysis becomes apparent: in telling their tales of woe, the restless ones relieve themselves of their pressures and anxieties and thus may free themselves of their bonds. If fear is the absence of information, as I have always held, then knowledge is indeed the presence of understanding. Or view it the other way round, if you prefer. Because of my books, people often call on me to help them understand problems of this nature. Whenever someone has seen a ghost or heard noises of a human kind that do not seem to go with a body, and feel it might be something I ought to look into, I usually do.

To be sure, I don't always find a ghost. But I frequently do find one, and moreover, I find that many of those who have had the uncanny experiences are themselves mediumistic, and are therefore capable of being communications vehicles for the discarnates. It is more common than most people realize, and really quite natural and harmless.

At times, it is sad and shocking, as all human suffering is; for man is his worst enemy, whether in the flesh or outside of it. But there is nothing mystical about the powers of ESP or the ability to experience ghostly phenomena.

There is nothing "out there" that is not essentially human— good, evil, or in-between. No Devil. No monsters. But once in a while the remnants of unfinished business, great anger, great hatred, can turn someone who has died into a psychotic entity. When an outsider, an "innocent bystander," happens to enter its world by moving into what used to be the disturbed deceased's home, place of work, or place of death, the spirit can be perceived as a threat—very real, menacing, even deadly.

And in some cases, it is. The terror in the night can cause psychological harm through excessive fear, or even bodily harm through a stroke or other physical reaction. It is the stuff that horrifying midnight tales are made of, especially when the story is true.

A ghost hunter who is afraid of ghosts isn't going to be much good. On the other hand, a self-styled expert who *thinks* he knows what to do when he is confronted with a ghostly manifestation may do more harm than good. Demonologists, vampire specialists, and exorcists may be having fun at the expense of their clients, those in true need of help. With a trained parapsychologist in charge of the case, chances are it will be resolved and the fear of the unknown will turn into the experience of a lifetime.

Scoffers like to dismiss all ghostly encounters by cutting the witnesses down to size—their size. The witnesses are probably mentally unbalanced, they say, or sick people who hallucinate a lot, or they were tired that day, or it must have been the reflection from (pick your light source), or finally, in desperation, they may say yes, something probably happened to them, but in the telling they blew it all up so you can't be sure any more what really happened.

I love the way many people who cannot accept the possibility of ghosts being real toss out their views on what happened to strangers. "Probably this or that," and from "probably," for them, it is only a short step to "certainly." The human mind is as clever at inventing away as it is at hallucinating. The advantage in being a scientifically trained reporter, as I am, is the ability to dismiss people's interpretations and find the facts themselves. A few years ago I talked of the *Ghosts I've Met* in a book that bore that title. Even more fascinating are the people I've met who encounter ghosts. Are they sick, unbalanced, crackpots whose testimony is worthless?

Far from it.

Those who fall into that category never get to me in the first place. They don't stand up under my methods of scrutiny. Crackpots, beware! Only after careful investigation and consideration of alternate explanations will I proceed with whatever measures are required to free the ghost from the living people. And the living people from the ghost.

In *Tales at Midnight*, I've selected my favorite true ghost stories, collected over my many years as a ghost hunter. These tales originally appeared in my earlier books, which are now quite difficult to get.

It is my hope that you find these tales entertaining as well as instructional. Here is a guided tour of the world that lies between life and the afterlife.

STAIRWAY OF FEAR

Some visitations from the Great Beyond are so powerful and horrible they can never be forgotten, especially when the entity follows one from the house just left in panic, to a new home, miles away, supposedly safe from it! But that is exactly what happened to the Manner family.

Somerset is one of those nondescript small towns that abound in rural Pennsylvania and that boast nothing more exciting than a few thousand homes, a few churches, a club or two and a lot of hardworking people whose lives pass under pretty ordinary and often drab circumstances. Those who leave may go on to better things in the big cities of the East, and those who stay have the comparative security of being among their own and living out their lives peacefully. But then there are those who leave not because they want to but because they are driven, driven by forces greater than themselves that they cannot resist.

The Manners are middle-aged people with two children, a fourteen-year-old son and a six-year-old daughter. The husband ran a television and radio shop which gave them an average income, neither below middle-class standards for a small town, nor much above it. Although Catholic, they did not consider themselves particularly religious. Mrs. Manner's people originally came from Austria, so there was enough European background in the family to give their lives a slight continental tinge, but other than that, they were and are typical Pennsylvania people without the slightest interest in, or knowledge of, such sophisticated matters as psychic research.

Of course, the occult was never unknown to Mrs. Manner. She was born with a veil over her eyes, which to many means the Second Sight. Her ability to see things before they happened was not "precognition" to her, but merely a special talent she took in her stride. One night she had a vivid dream about her son, then miles away in the army. She vividly saw him walking down a hall in a bathrobe, with blood running down his leg. Shortly after she awakened the next day, she was notified that her son had been attacked by a rattlesnake and, when found, was near death. One night she awoke to see an image of her sister standing beside her bed. There was nothing fearful about the apparition, but she was dressed all in black.

The next day that sister died.

But these instances did not frighten Mrs. Manner; they were glimpses into eternity and nothing more.

As the years went by, the Manners accumulated enough funds to look for a more comfortable home than the one they were occupying, and as luck—or fate—would have it, one day in 1966 they were offered a fine, old house in one of the better parts of town. The house seemed in excellent condition; it had the appearance of a Victorian home with all the lovely touches of that bygone era about it. It had stood empty for two years, and since it belonged to an estate, the executors seemed anxious to finally sell the house. The Manners made no special inquiries about their projected new home simply because everything seemed so right and pleasant. The former owners had been wealthy people, they were informed, and had lavished much money and love on the house.

When the price was quoted to them, the Manners looked at each other in disbelief. It was far below what they had expected for such a splendid house. "We'll take it," they said, almost in unison, and soon the house was theirs.

"Why do you suppose we got it for such a ridiculously low price?" Mr. Manner mused, but his wife could only shrug. To her, that was not at all important. She never believed one should look a gift horse in the mouth.

It was late summer when they finally moved into their newly acquired home. Hardly had they been installed when Mrs. Manner knew there was something not right with the place.

From the very first, she had felt uncomfortable in it, but being a sensible person, she had put it down to being in a new and unaccustomed place. But as this feeling persisted she realized that she was being *watched* by some unseen force all the time, day and night, and her nerves began to tense under the strain.

The very first night she spent in the house, she was aroused at exactly two o'clock in the morning, seemingly for no reason. Her hair stood up on her arms and chills shook her body. Again, she put this down to having worked so hard getting the new home into shape.

But the "witching hour" of 2 A.M. kept awakening her with the same uncanny feeling that something was wrong, and instinctively she knew it was not her, or someone in her family, who was in trouble, but the new house.

With doubled vigor, she put all her energies into polishing furniture and getting the rooms into proper condition. That way, she was very tired and hoped to sleep through the night. But no matter how physically exhausted she was, at two o'clock the uncanny feeling woke her.

The first week somehow passed despite this eerie feeling, and Monday rolled around again. In the bright light of the late summer day, the house somehow seemed friendlier and her fears of the night had vanished.

She was preparing breakfast in the kitchen for her children that Monday morning. As she was buttering a piece of toast for her little girl, she happened to glance up toward the doorway. There, immaculately dressed, *stood a man.* The stranger, she noticed, wore shiny black shoes, navy blue pants, and a white shirt. She even made out his tie, saw it was striped, and then went on to observe the man's face. The picture was so clear she could make out the way the man's snowy white hair was parted.

Her immediate reaction was that he had somehow entered the house and she was about to say hello, when it occurred to her that she had not heard the opening of a door or any other sound—no footfalls, no steps.

"Look," she said to her son, whose back was turned to the apparition, but by the time her children turned around, the man was gone like a puff of smoke.

Mrs. Manner was not too frightened by what she had witnessed, although she realized her visitor had not been of the flesh and blood variety. When she told her husband about it that evening, he laughed.

Ghosts, indeed!

The matter would have rested there had it not been for the fact that the very next day something else happened. Mrs. Manner was on her way into the kitchen from the backyard of the house, when she suddenly saw a woman go past her refrigerator. This time the materialization was not as perfect. Only half of the body was visible, but she noticed her shoes, dress up to the knees, and that the figure seemed in a hurry.

This still did not frighten her, but she began to wonder. All those eerie feelings seemed to add up now. What had they gotten themselves into by buying this house? No wonder it was so cheap. It was haunted!

Mrs. Manner was a practical person, the uncanny experiences notwithstanding, or perhaps because of them. They had paid good money for the house and no specters were going to dislodge them!

But the fight had just begun. A strange kind of web began to envelop her frequently, as if some unseen force were trying to wrap her into a wet, cold blanket. When she touched the "web," there was nothing to be seen or felt, and yet, the clammy, cold force was still with her. *A strange scent of flowers* manifested itself out of nowhere and followed her from room to room. Soon her husband smelled it too, and his laughing stopped. He, too, became concerned: their children must not be frightened by whatever it was that was present in the house.

It soon was impossible to keep doors locked. No matter how often they would lock a door in the house, it was found wide open soon afterwards, the locks turned by unseen hands. One center of particular activities was the old china closet, and the scent of flowers was especially strong in its vicinity.

"What are we going to do about this?" Mrs. Manner asked her husband one night. They decided to find out more about the house, as a starter. They had hesitated to mention anything about their plight out of fear of being ridiculed or thought unbalanced. In a small town, people don't like to talk about ghosts.

The first person Mrs. Manner turned to was a neighbor who

had lived down the street for many years. When she noticed that the neighbor did not pull back at the mention of weird goings-on in the house, but, to the contrary, seemed genuinely interested, Mrs. Manner poured out her heart and described what she had seen.

In particular, she took great pains to describe the two apparitions. The neighbor nodded gravely.

"It's them, all right," she said, and started to fill Mrs. Manner in on the history of their house. This was the first time Mrs. Manner had heard of it and the description of the man she had seen tallied completely with the appearance of the man who had owned the house before.

"He died here," the neighbor explained. "They really loved their home, he and his wife. The old lady never wanted to leave or sell it."

"But what do you make of the strange scent of flowers?" Mrs. Manner asked.

"The old lady loved flowers, had fresh ones in the house every day."

Relieved to know what it was all about, but hardly happy at the prospect of sharing her house with ghosts, Mrs. Manner then went to see the chief of police in the hope of finding some way of getting rid of her unwanted "guests."

The chief scratched his head.

"Ghosts?" he said, not at all jokingly. "You've got me there. That's not my territory."

But he promised to send an extra patrol around in case it was just old-fashioned burglars.

Mrs. Manner thanked him and left. She knew otherwise and realized the police would not be able to help her.

She decided they had to learn to live with their ghosts, especially as the latter had been in the house before them. Perhaps it wouldn't be so bad after all, she mused, now that they knew who it was that would not leave.

Perhaps one could even become friendly, sort of one big,

happy family, half people, half ghosts? But she immediately rejected the notion. What about the children? So far, they had not *seen* them, but they knew of the doors that wouldn't stay shut and the other uncanny phenomena.

Fortunately, Mrs. Manner did not understand the nature of poltergeists. Had she realized that the very presence of her teen-age son was in part responsible for the physical nature of the happenings, she would no doubt have sent him away. But the phenomena continued unabated, day and night.

One night at dinner, with everyone accounted for, an enormous crash shook the house. It felt as if a ton of glass had fallen on the kitchen floor. When they rushed into the kitchen, they found everything in order, nothing misplaced.

At this point, Mrs. Manner fell back on her early religious world.

"Maybe we should call the minister?" she suggested, and no sooner said than done. The following day, the minister came to their house. When he had heard their story, he nodded quietly and said a silent prayer for the souls of the disturbed ones.

He had a special reason to do so, it developed. They had been among his parishioners when alive. In fact, he had been to their home for dinner many times, and the house was familiar to him despite the changes the present owners had made.

If anyone could, surely their own minister should be able to send those ghosts away.

Not by a long shot.

Either the couple did not put much stock into their minister's powers, or the pull of the house was stronger, but the phenomena continued. In fact, after the minister had tried to exorcise the ghosts, things got worse.

Many a night, the Manners ran out into the street when lights kept going on and off by themselves. Fortunately, the children slept through all this, but how long would they remain unaffected?

At times, the atmosphere was so thick Mrs. Manner could not get near the breakfast nook in the kitchen to clear the table.

Enveloped by the strong vibrations, she felt herself tremble and on two occasions fainted and was thus found by her family.

They were seriously considering moving now, and letting the original "owners" have the house again. They realized now that the house had never been truly "empty" for those two years the real estate man had said it was not in use.

It was 2 A.M. when they finally went up to bed.

Things felt worse than ever before. Mrs. Manner clearly sensed *three* presences with her now and started to cry.

"I'm leaving this house," she exclaimed. "You can have it back!" Her husband had gone ahead of her up the stairs to get the bedding from the linen closet. She began to follow him and slowly went up the stairs. After she had climbed about half way up, something forced her to turn around and look back.

What she saw has remained with her ever since, deeply impressed in her mind with the acid of stark fear.

Down below her on the stairway, was a big, burly man, trying to pull himself up the stairs.

His eyes were red with torture as he tried to talk to her.

Evidently he had been hurt, for his trousers and shirt were covered with mud. Or was it dried blood?

He was trying to hang on to the banister and held his hands out towards her.

"Oh, God, it can't be true," she thought and went up a few more steps. Then she dared look down again.

The man was still holding out his hand in a desperate move to get her attention. When she failed to respond, he threw it down in a gesture of impatience and frustration.

With a piercing scream, she ran up the stairs to her husband, weeping out of control.

The house had been firmly locked and no one could have gained entrance. Not that they thought the apparitions were flesh and blood people. The next morning, no trace of the nocturnal phenomenon could be found on the stairs. It was as if it had never happened.

But that morning, the Manners decided to pack and get out fast. "I want no more houses," Mrs. Manner said firmly, and so they bought a trailer. Meanwhile, they lived in an apartment.

But their furniture and all their belongings were still in the house, and it was necessary to go back a few more times to get them. They thought that since they had signed over the deed, it would be all right for them to go back. After all, it was no longer *their* house.

As Mrs. Manner cautiously ascended the stairs, she was still trembling with fear. Any moment now, the specter might confront her again. But all seemed calm. Suddenly, the scent of flowers was with her again and she knew the ghosts were still in residence.

As if to answer her doubts, the doors to the china closet flew open at that moment.

Although she wanted nothing further to do with the old house, Mrs. Manner made some more inquiries. The terrible picture of the tortured man on the stairs did not leave her mind. Who was he, and what could she have done for him?

Then she heard that the estate wasn't really settled, the children were still fighting over it. Was that the reason the parents could not leave the house in peace? Was the man on the stairs someone who needed help, someone who had been hurt in the house?

"Forget it," the husband said, and they stored most of their furniture. The new house trailer would have no bad vibrations and they could travel wherever they wanted, if necessary.

After they had moved into the trailer, they heard rumors that the new owners of their house had encountered problems also. But they did not care to hear about them and studiously stayed away from the house. That way, they felt, the ghosts would avoid them also, now that they were back in what used to be their beloved home!

But a few days later, Mrs. Manner noticed a strange scent of flowers wafting through her brand-new trailer. Since she had not bought any flowers, nor opened a perfume bottle, it puzzled her. Then, with a sudden impact that was almost crushing, she knew where and when she had smelled this scent before. It was the personal scent of the ghostly woman in the old house! Had she followed her here into the trailer?

When she discussed this new development with her husband that night, they decided to fumigate the trailer, air it and get rid of the scent, if they could. Somehow they thought they might be mistaken and it was just coincidence. But the scent remained, clear and strong, and the feeling of a presence that came with it soon convinced them that they had not yet seen the last of the Somerset ghosts.

They sold the new trailer and bought another house, a fifty-seven-year-old, nice rambling home in a nearby Pennsylvania town called Stoystown, far enough from Somerset to give them the hope that the Unseen Ones would not be able to follow them there.

Everything was fine after they had moved their furniture in and for the first time in many a month, the Manners could relax. About two months after they had moved to Stoystown, the scent of flowers returned. Now it was accompanied by another smell, that resembling burned matches.

The Manners were terrified. Was there no escape from the Uncanny? A few days later, Mrs. Manner observed a smoky form rise up in the house. Nobody had been smoking. The form roughly resembled the vague outlines of a human being.

Her husband, fortunately, experienced the smells also, so she was not alone in her plight. But the children, who had barely shaken off their terror, were now faced with renewed fears. They could not keep running—running away from what?

They tried every means at their command. Holy water, incense, a minister's prayer, their own prayers, curses and commands to the Unseen: but the scent remained.

Gradually, they learned to live with their psychic problems. For a mother possessed of definite mediumistic powers from youth and a young adult in the household are easy prey to those among the restless dead who desire a continued life of earthly activities. With the physical powers drawn from these living people, they play and continue to exist in a world of which they are no longer a part.

As the young man grew older, the available power dwindled and the scent was noticed less frequently. But the tortured man on the stairs of the house in Somerset will have to wait for a more willing medium to set him free.

THE HOUSE OF THE DEAD

Mrs. G. threw a hasty look toward the third floor window of the modest wooden house on Mountview Place set back a few paces from the street. Then she shuddered and quickly hurried past, without looking back. Mrs. G. knew that was the best way to pass *that* house.

Everyone in the neighborhood knew the house was haunted and there was no point in seeing things one wasn't supposed to. Still—if the figure at the window was there, perhaps a glance would not hurt. It was a question of curiosity versus fear of the unknown, and fear won out.

The house itself looks like a typical lower-middle-class dwelling built around the turn of the century. White sides are trimmed in green, and a couple of steps lead up to the entrance door. Its three stories—you can call the third floor an attic, if you prefer—look no different than the floors in any of the smaller houses in suburban Pittsburgh. There is an appropriately sized backyard to the rear of the house, with some bushes and flowers. And there are houses to both sides of this one. The block is quiet with very little traffic running through it. By car, it is about forty minutes from downtown Pittsburgh, and most people don't go there more than maybe once in a while to shop. Life on Mountview Place is unexciting and drab and if it weren't for people like Mrs. G. worrying about the third floor window, nobody would even notice the house. But things were a little different when it was new and the neighborhood was a lot more rustic than it is now.

The early history of the house is somewhat shrouded, except that it was already in existence exactly as it looks today at the turn of the century. At that time Mr. Allshouse, the local plumber—he has his own shop and is in his late sixties now—was only a mere child. So he did not know the strange man who came to live in the house until many years later. But in 1908, a Hollander named Vander bought the house and he and his family lived in it until his wife died. In 1953 he left the house, and thereby hangs the first part of this strange tale. Although there were three children in the Vander family, he evidently had decided not to remain where his wife had died, but we can't be altogether sure as to why he left. In later years Mr. Allshouse and Vander had become friends, and even after his wife's passing Vander maintained contact with the plumber.

One day Allshouse was walking toward the house when he met Vander's niece en route. They stopped to chat and he mentioned where he was going. "Then you don't know?" the niece intoned. "My uncle has been dead for a month."

This came as a surprise to the plumber and he wondered how the otherwise hale and hearty Hollander had died so suddenly. He remembered well their initial meeting. This was several years ago, when Vander had needed some repairs done in the house. The work completed, the plumber presented his bill. Mr. Vander asked him to wait.

"Don't believe much in banks," he explained. "You don't mind taking cash, do you?"

"Not at all," the plumber assured him. The Dutchman then walked up the already shaky stairs to the attic. Allshouse could clearly hear him walk about up there as if he were moving some heavy object around, looking for something. Then the sound of a drawer closing was heard, and soon after, the Dutchman's heavy footsteps came down the stairs again.

"Here's your money," he said and smiled. He was a friendly man who didn't mind a chat with strangers. After a minute or two of discussing the state of the world and the weather in Pittsburgh in particular, the two men parted.

And now the Hollander was dead. It seemed very strange to the plumber. Why had Vander left the comfortable house just before his death and what was to happen to the house now?

Two weeks went by and other matters occupied the plumber's mind. He was walking down Trenton Avenue one afternoon, when he looked up and who should be trotting towards him but Mr. Vander!

Without thinking, the plumber called out a friendly "Hello!" The man did not react, so Allshouse shouted, "Mr. Vander! Mr. Vander!"

At this the man, who had meanwhile passed him, turned, smiled rather wanly, and said, "Hello."

But he did not stop to chat as he had always done before, and it seemed strange that this time Vander was cool and distant when normally he had been so friendly.

Long after Mr. Vander had disappeared in the opposite direction, the plumber wondered why his friend had behaved so strangely. Then it suddenly hit him that the man had been dead and buried for six weeks.

Prior to his death Vander had sold the house to a couple named McBride. Apparently it was a private transaction, for no one knows exactly how it happened, or even why, but the McBrides were installed in the house by the time Mr. Vander passed on . . . or at least part of the way on.

The McBrides had no children, and Mrs. McBride was crippled, having once fallen in an alley. Consequently she dragged one leg in a rather pronounced manner when walking.

Around 1964, Mrs. McBride died, leaving the house to her husband, Franklin. Soon after, Mr. McBride's usual calm behavior changed rapidly. Where he had hardly been known for any eccentricities in the neighborhood, he seemed now a subject for discussion up and down the street. For one thing, he soon refused to go upstairs under any circumstances, and made his bed in an old Morris chair in the front parlor downstairs.

On more than one occasion, neighbors saw the man run out into the street in a state of abject fear. Not understanding his reasons, gossip blamed it on alcohol, but the fact is Mr. McBride never drank anything at all.

Ultimately, his sister-in-law, a Mrs. Naugle, had him placed in the state mental institution at Torrence, where he is still living.

The power of attorney then passed into her hands, and it was she who rented the house to the Kennedy family. For about a year the house had stood empty after Mr. McBride's forced departure. In that time, dust had gathered and the house looked eerie even in the daytime. But at night people absolutely refused to walk close by it and even sensible people would rather cross the street than face walking close to its windows. Mrs. Evelyn Kennedy had not heard anything special about the house one way or the other.

It seemed like the kind of house she wanted for her brood and so she and her husband rented it in 1965. For almost a year the Kennedys lived quietly in the house on Mountview Place and kept busy with the ordinary routines of daily living. There was, first of all, Mrs. Evelyn Kennedy herself, a portly lady of mixed Irish-German ancestry, as so many are in this area, age forty-five and a lively and articulate housewife. At one time she had operated a beauty parlor downtown but now she was much too busy for that. Some of her equipment was still in the attic and on occasion she would perform her erstwhile duties for members of the family or friends there.

Mr. Wilbert Kennedy managed a nearby gas station. Five years her senior, he was a wiry, quiet-spoken man who was rarely around the house, the nature of his business being one of long hours.

Of their four children, two were married and lived away from home. The other two daughters, Claudia and Penny, lived with their parents. Claudia was married, but her husband had disappeared, and at twenty-four, she was kept busy with her two children, Debra, then seven, and Maria, then one year old. Penny, unmarried, was eighteen at the time they moved into the house. Except for an occasional friend, this was the entire cast of characters in the strange tale that was about to unfold.

On July 7, 1966, the landlady, Mrs. Naugle, decided she wanted to sell the house. Actually, it belonged to her brother-in-law in the institution but she had power of attorney so there was really nothing to stop her. Why she suddenly decided to sell, no one but she knew and she is hardly likely to tell us. But the very same real estate dealer, a man named McKnight, who had gotten the

Kennedys into the house, was now entrusted with the disposal of the house to a new owner. Where this would leave the tenants no one knew or cared.

Actually, selling the house should not have proved too difficult. It was reasonably well kept, had an attractive exterior and a nice, large backyard, and the block was quiet and tree-lined. The downstairs parlor was separated from the dining room by a heavy oaken double door that could be pulled back entirely to make the downstairs into one large room, if one had many guests. To the right was the staircase which led straight up two flights. The second story contained the bedrooms and the third floor, actually the attic, was occupied by an additional bedroom in front and a large "rear room" which Mrs. Kennedy had filled with the remnants of her beauty parlor days and sundry suitcases, boxes, and the sort of things people have placed into attics ever since houses were built with them. The house was eminently suitable for any family with children.

Although the For Sale sign was up outside their home, the Kennedys continued with their daily business. Somehow they felt it would be some time before the house would be sold and then, perhaps, to an owner who did not wish to live in it. Why worry?

Penny, a determined young lady, had decided she preferred the privacy of the attic to the family presence on the second floor and moved her bed to the empty bedroom in the attic. The day after the For Sale sign had been installed outside, she came down to use the bathroom.

When she went back up to the attic, she found her way barred by a woman standing at the window. Since it was broad daylight, Penny had ample opportunity to look her over. She was an elderly woman with gray hair, wearing a somewhat unusual amount of rouge on her face. Her blue dress was like a long robe. In her hands she held some beads, and when Penny noticed her, the woman held out her arms toward her, all the while smiling at her. But Penny did not feel friendly at all. She knew there couldn't possibly be anyone of flesh-and-blood standing there.

She let out a scream and rushed down the stairs, almost falling in the process.

Within hours, she was back in her old room on the second floor, and ten horses wouldn't get her up into the attic again.

But her troubles were far from over even on the second floor. The water kept turning itself on day and night. Her alarm clock was unplugged. Jewelry disappeared and could not be found despite careful and exhaustive search. The next day it would be back at the same spot from which it disappeared.

Soon the phenomena spread to other members of the family. Mrs. Evelyn Kennedy, suffering from arthritis and a bad heart, would sometimes be unable to bend down because of swollen legs. One day she found herself all alone in the house. Her shoes were always kept under a chest of drawers in the bedroom. That day the shoes had somehow been pushed too far back under the chest and she could not reach them.

"Oh my," she said out loud. "I wish I could get at my shoes. What shall I do?"

With that she entered her bathroom for a shower. Afterwards, as she opened the bathroom door, the door hit something solid. She looked down. Someone had placed her shoes, which a few minutes before had been under the chest of drawers in her room, in front of the bathroom door. Yet, she was alone in the house.

Mrs. Kennedy put two and two together. Who was the woman in the blue robe that had frightened her daughter Penny?

Cautiously, she called the landlady, Mrs. Naugle, and explained what had happened.

"Oh my God," the lady sighed, "that sounds just like my sister. She was laid out in a blue robe."

But she would not discuss this any further. It upset her, and she wanted no part of it.

Shortly after, Mrs. Kennedy was ironing downstairs in the parlor. All of a sudden a heavy object shot out of the door jamb and narrowly missed her. She stopped working and examined the object. It was a homemade pin of some sort. When she showed it to the landlady, the latter turned away, advising her to destroy the object. It was even harder to talk about the house after that incident.

Sobbing sounds were soon heard in the dining room when it was completely empty. Up in the attic the family would hear the sound of someone dragging legs, someone crippled, and they remembered in terror how the late Mrs. McBride had been thus afflicted. Was this her ghost, they wondered.

They had scarcely enough time to worry about what to do about all this that had suddenly burst upon them, when Mrs. Kennedy got to talking to the mailman, a Mr. Packen, who lived nearby. Somehow the talk turned to psychic phenomena and the mailman nodded gravely.

"I seen her, too," he confided. "I seen her sweeping the pavement. Right in front of the house. I seen her."

"Who have you seen?" asked Mrs. Kennedy, as if she didn't know.

"Who but that lady, Mrs. McBride?" the mailman answered. "Big as life she was."

He in turn had been no stranger to this sort of thing. In his own house down the street he once saw a little old lady who seemed strangely familiar. As a mailman, he knows most of his "customers" well enough and the little old lady in his house rang a bell.

"What are you doing in my house?" he demanded. "You're supposed to be dead!"

Reproachfully he glanced at her and she nodded sadly and dissolved into the evening mist.

So it wasn't particularly shocking for him to hear about the goings-on at the Kennedy house.

The little old lady who had visited the mailman apparently had some business of her own, and as it is unfinished business that keeps these denizens of the netherworld from going on into the Great Beyond, he wondered what it was she had wanted.

One afternoon, Debra was playing in the downstairs parlor,

when she felt herself not alone. In looking she saw a little old lady standing in the room. Wearing black clothes, she seemed strangely old-fashioned and unreal to her, but there was no doubt in Debra's mind that she had a visitor. While she rose to meet the stranger, the woman disappeared. Having heard of her Aunt Penny's encounter with the lady on the stairs, she knew at once that this was not the same person. Whereas the lady on the stairs had been tall and smiling, this woman was short and bent and quizzical in her expression.

The excitement of this vision had hardly died down when Mrs. Kennedy found her work in the kitchen, washing dishes, interrupted by the feeling that she was about to have a visitor. Since she was alone in the house at the moment, she immediately proceeded to the front door to open it. Without thinking anything special, she opened the front door and standing there and waiting was a lady. She was short of stature, her dress had big, puffed sleeves, she wore gloves and carried a big black umbrella. Mrs. Kennedy also noticed a golden pin and the bustle of her dress. In particular, she was astonished to see her hat, which was large and had a big bill on it—something no woman today would wear.

As she still wondered who this strange woman might be, she motioned to her to come in, which the woman did, brushing past her. Only then did it occur to Mrs. Kennedy that she had not heard the doorbell ring! Turning around and going after her visitor, she found that no one had come in.

Now she, too, realized that it was someone other than the late Mrs. McBride, if indeed it was she, who kept coming to the house. It was the mailman's friend; strange as it might seem, but from the description she was sure it was the same person.

The mystery deepened even further when Debra reported seeing a man in the kitchen at a time when no man was in the house. The man had worn a blue shirt and brown pants, but they were not the sort of clothes worn by people today. He stood in a corner of the kitchen as if he belonged there and though Debra was frightened, she managed to see enough of the wraith before he faded away again.

It was a Monday night some weeks after this experience, that Claudia and Penny were on the stairs alone. Mr. Kennedy and the two grandchildren were already in bed in their rooms. All the lights were out and only the street lights cast a reflection of sorts into the house through the windows. Suddenly the two girls heard the sound of someone running from the kitchen toward the living room. They looked up and what they saw made their blood turn to ice; there in the dim light of the kitchen stood the outline of a very large man. *With a huge leap, he came after them.* Faster than lightning, they ran up the stairs, with the shadowy man in hot pursuit. As they looked back in sheer terror, they saw him coming, but he stopped at the landing. Then he was gone, just disappeared like a puff of smoke.

From that moment on, the two young women refused to stay downstairs at night.

The downstairs parlor was as "unsafe" from the incursions of the ghosts as was the attic, and before long even the backyard was no longer free from whatever it was that wanted attention. It was almost as if the unseen forces were engaged in a campaign of mounting terror to drive home the feeling that the Kennedy's were not in possession of the house: *the ghosts were.*

Lights would go on and off by themselves. Water started to gush in the bathroom and when they investigated they found someone unseen had turned the tap on. Late at night, they often heard someone cry softly in their backyard. Enough light from the windows illuminated that plot of land to assure them that it was no human agent. They huddled together, frightened, desolate, and yet unwilling to give up the house which they truly loved. The attic was particularly active during those weeks immediately following the landlady's decision to sell their house. Someone was moving heavy furniture around there at night—or so it sounded. Nothing ever was changed in the morning. Mrs.

THE HOUSE OF THE DEAD

Kennedy sought the advice of a good friend, Mrs. Lucille Hags, who had been to the house often.

One evening when things had been particularly active, Evelyn Kennedy dialed her friend. The soothing voice at the other end of the phone momentarily calmed her. But then she clearly heard someone else dialing her phone.

"Are you dialing?" she asked her friend, but Mrs. Hags had not touched her telephone either. Perhaps there had been some kind of cross-connection. Mrs. Kennedy decided to ignore it and bravely started to tell her friend what had happened that evening at the house.

"I wonder if it has something to do with Mrs. McBride," she ventured. No sooner had she said this, when heavy breathing, the breath of someone very close by, struck her ear.

"Do you hear that?" she asked, somewhat out of breath now herself.

"Yes, I did," said Mrs. Hags. Six times the heavy breathing interfered with their telephone conversation during the following weeks. Each time it started the moment either of them mentioned the phenomena in the house. Was one of their ghostly tenants listening in? So it would seem. The telephone people assured Mrs. Kennedy there was nothing wrong with her line.

Nothing wrong? she asked herself. Everything was wrong; the house was all wrong and what were they to do?

One sunny morning she decided to fight back. After all, this had been their happy home for a while now and no phantoms were going to drive them out of it. She tried to reason it out but no matter how many of the noises she could explain by ordinary causes, so many things remained that simply could not be explained away. There were, as far as she could make out three ghosts in the house. The two women and the heavy-set man. She wasn't quite sure who the man was, and yet it seemed to her it must be the Hollander, Vander, whose money had always been hidden up there in the attic. Had he returned for it, or was he simply staying on because he didn't like the way he left? Those were the questions racing through Mrs. Kennedy's mind often now.

To be sure, at least one of the *stay-behinds* was friendly.

There was the time Mrs. Kennedy slipped on the stairs and was about to fall headlong down the whole flight of stairs. It was a warm summer day and she was alone at home, so that she would have lain there helpless had she injured herself. But something kept her from falling! Some force stronger than gravity held on to her skirts and pulled her back onto her feet. It wasn't her imagination and it wasn't a supreme effort of her own that did it. She was already half into the air, falling, when she was yanked back, upright.

Shortly after, she managed to repair to the attic, where her hair-drying equipment was stored. As she sat there, resting, she suddenly felt something wet and cold across her legs. She reached down only to feel a soft, moist mass that dissolved rapidly at her touch! This was enough to give her the willies, and she began to fear for her life because of her bad heart.

And yet, when the prospective buyers came more frequently to look at the house, and it seemed that the house might be sold after all, she found herself turning to her ghostly protector.

"Please, Mrs. McBride," she prayed silently, "don't let her sell the house!"

As if by a miracle, the most interested buyer who had been close to a decision in favor of taking the house, went away and was never seen again. The house remained unsold. Coincidence? If there be such things, perhaps. But not to Mrs. Kennedy.

She did not particularly care to have word of their predicament get around. It was bad enough to have ghosts, but to be known as a haunted family was even worse. And yet how could it be avoided? It wasn't just she and her two daughters who experienced these strange things.

Even her husband, who wasn't exactly given to belief in ghosts, was impressed when he saw a chair move from under a desk by its own force. He tried it several times afterwards, hoping he could duplicate the phenomena by merely stomping his feet or gently touching the chair, but it required full force to move it.

The insurance man who had been servicing them for years was just as doubtful about the whole thing when he heard about it.

"No such thing as a ghost," he commented as he stood in the hallway. At this moment the banister started to vibrate to such an extent they thought it would explode. He grabbed his hat and took his doubts to the nearest bar.

Sandra, a friend, had been sitting with Mrs. Kennedy downstairs not long ago, when suddenly she clearly heard someone in the bedroom overhead, the footsteps of someone running across it.

"I didn't know you had other company," she remarked to Mrs. Kennedy.

"I don't," Mrs. Kennedy answered dryly, and the friend left, somewhat faster than she had planned.

Penny, 21 years old, and single, turned out to be more psychic than any of them. Hardly had she recovered from her terrible experience on the stairs, when something even more unspeakable occurred.

One evening, as she was retiring for the night, and had the lights turned off in her room, she felt something cold lie down in bed beside her. With a scream she jumped out and switched the lights back on. There was nothing, but a chill still pervaded the entire area!

In the summer of 1967, Penny found herself alone on the stairs on one occasion, when she suddenly heard a voice speak to her.

"It's all right . . . she can come out now," some woman said somewhere in back of her. There was no one visible who could have spoken these words and no one nearby. Besides, it was not a voice she recognized. It sounded strangely hollow and yet imperious at the same time. Someone was giving an order, but who, and to whom? Clearly, this someone still considered herself mistress of this house.

Although Penny had no interest in psychic matters, she wondered about these phenomena. Who was the man she had seen on the stairs? Who was the woman whose voice she had heard?

Somewhere she read an advertisement for a pendulum as an aid to psychic perception. As soon as it had come in the mail, she retired to her room and tried it out.

Holding the pendulum over a piece of board, she intoned, more in jest than for serious research reasons, "Mr. Vander, are you here?"

With a swift move, the pendulum was ripped from her hands and landed clear across the room. She hadn't used it since, nor did she really care if Mr. Vander was the ghost she saw. She just wanted to be left alone.

The summer passed, and it was September, 1967, that Mrs. Kennedy realized there was more to this triangle of ghosts than just their presence. She was standing outside the house, chatting with a neighbor.

"Are the children having a party?" the neighbor asked.

"Why, no," she replied, knowing full well the children were all out of the house at the moment.

She was wondering why her neighbor had asked such a peculiar question, and was about to say so, when she heard a loud noise coming from the empty house: it sounded indeed as if a group of children were having a party upstairs, running up and down in the house. All she could do was shrug and turn away.

Maria, the three-year-old, is a precocious youngster who speaks better than her years would call for. One day she accompanied her grandmother to the attic. While Mrs. Kennedy was busy with her chores in the front room, the little girl played in the rear of the attic. Suddenly she came running out of the back room and beckoned her grandmother to follow her.

"There is a nice lady back there and she likes me," she explained.

Immediately Mrs. Kennedy went back but she saw nothing this time.

Whether this visit to the attic had stirred up some sort of

psychic contact, or whether her growing years now allowed her to express herself more clearly, the little girl had something more to say about the ghosts before long. Naturally, no one discussed such matters with her. Why frighten the child?

"There is a little boy in the attic," Maria explained earnestly, "and his name is Yackie. He died up there. He plays snowball out the window because he isn't allowed out of the attic."

At first these stories were dismissed as the fantasies of a child. Mrs. Kennedy was even a bit amused about the way Maria said "Yackie" instead of Jackie. They did not wish to stop her from telling this story over and over, out of fear that repressing her might make it more interesting. But as the weeks went on the little girl developed a strange affinity for the attic, especially the rear portion.

"Why are you always running up there, Maria?" her grandmother finally asked.

"Because," the little girl said, and became agitated, "because there is a man up there. Yackie told me about him."

"What about this man?"

"He died. He was shot in the head and all of his blood came out and he's buried in the backyard under the bushes."

"Why was he shot in the head, child?" the grandmother asked, almost as if she believed the story.

"Because he was crazy and he cried, that's why," the child replied. Her grandmother was silent for a moment, trying to sort things out.

Could a three-year-old make up such a yarn? she wondered.

"Come," the little girl said, and took her by the hand, "I'll show you." She led Mrs. Kennedy to the dining room window and pointed at the bushes in their backyard.

"It's under the bushes there," Maria repeated and stared out the window.

Mrs. Kennedy shuddered. It was a spot she had wondered about many times. No matter how she tried, no matter what she planted, *nothing would grow on that spot!*

But as it turned colder, the house seemed to settle down and the disturbances faded away. True, no one came to inquire about buying it either. The Kennedys half believed their troubles might just have faded away, both their worldly and their unworldly difficulties.

They thought less and less about them and a spark of hope returned to Mrs. Kennedy about staying on at the house. She tried to make some discreet inquiries about the former owners of the house and even attempted to find the official records and deeds of sale. But her efforts were thwarted on all sides. Neighbors suddenly turned pale and would not discuss the matter. Nobody admitted knowing anything at all about the Hollander, Mr. Vander. Why, for instance, had she been told he left no children when he died? Only accidentally did she discover that there were three children. Was one of them named Jackie perhaps? She could not be sure.

The winter came, and a bitterly cold winter it was. Late in January, her composure was rudely shattered when a representative of the real estate agent paid them a visit. The house was being offered for sale once again.

That day one of her married daughters was visiting Mrs. Kennedy. She had brought her baby along and needed some toys for it to play with. "Go up into the attic. There's plenty of stuff there," Mrs. Kennedy suggested.

The woman, accompanied by her sister Claudia, went up into the attic. She was barefoot and casually dressed. Suddenly, Claudia pushed her to one side. "Watch out," she said and pointed to the floor boards. There, stuck between two boards, with the cutting edge pointing up, was a single-edged razor blade.

Somewhat shaken by their experience, the two women went back downstairs, after having pulled the blade out of the floor with some difficulty. It had been shoved into the crack between the boards with considerable strength. Nobody in the house used single-edged razor blades. In fact, Mr. Kennedy, the only man in the house, used an electric shaver.

Suddenly, the activities started all over. The front door would continually open by itself and shut by itself, and there was never anyone there when someone went to check. This happened mainly at night and in each case Mrs. Kennedy found the door securely locked. The door she and the others heard open was not a physical door, apparently, but an echo from the past!

The Kennedys were patient for several days, then they decided that something had to be done. It was a nice house all right, but sooner or later someone would buy it, and they couldn't afford to buy it themselves, unfortunately. Since they could stop neither the landlady from trying to sell it, nor the ghostly inhabitants from playing in it, it was perhaps the wisest thing to look for another home.

By April they had finally found a nice house in nearby Penn Hills, and the moment they set foot in it they knew it would do fine.

With her deeply developed psychic sense Mrs. Kennedy also knew at once that she would have no problems with unseen visitors in *that* house.

It gave them a degree of pleasure to be moving out on their landlady rather than waiting to be evicted by the new owner. Gradually their belongings were moved to their new home.

On the last day, when almost everything had already been removed, Mrs. Kennedy, her husband, and their son, who had come to help them move, stood in the now almost empty house once more. There were still a few boxes left in the cellar. The two men went back into the cellar to get them out, while Mrs. Kennedy waited for them upstairs.

"Come," Mr. Kennedy said, and shivered in the spring air, "it's late. Let's finish up."

The clock of a nearby church started to strike twelve midnight.

They loaded the boxes into the car, carefully locked the front door of the house and then the garden gate.

At this precise moment, all three clearly heard the front door open and close again, and loud steps reverberate inside the empty house.

"There must be someone in there," Mrs. Kennedy's son murmured. He did not believe in ghosts and had always poo-pooed the tales told by his mother and sisters.

Quickly he unlocked the gate and front door once more and re-entered the dark house.

After a few moments, he returned, relocked house and gate and, somewhat sheepishly, shook his head.

"Nothing. It's all empty."

Not at all, Mrs. Kennedy thought, as the car pulled out into the night, not at all.

That was only the reception committee for the next tenant.

THE CURSED CASTLE

One of the strangest cases I have ever investigated took me from sunny California to the dank, dark recesses of an Austrian castle, a case so strange that I am still hard-put to find a parallel in the annals of psychic research.

It all began in Vienna in 1964, when my good friend Turhan Bey told me of a haunted castle belonging to a friend of his who resided in Hollywood. The friend's name was von Wurmbrand, and Turhan promised to introduce us. But somehow the matter slipped our minds at the time.

Fate, however, had meant for me to meet this man, apparently, for in November of the same year I received a letter from Count Wurmbrand, telling me he had read my book *Ghost Hunter* and thought that possibly I could help him solve his psychic problem. What had called me to his attention was not only my book but a newspaper article in the Vienna *Volksblatt*, a newspaper of very minor importance that had seen fit to ridicule my work. The article had dealt with the ghost at Forchtenstein reported by me in *Ghosts I've Met*.

Subsequently, I met the Count at the Hotel Roosevelt in Hollywood. Over lunch, we talked of his predicament and I promised to come to Steyersberg, his ancestral castle, that very summer. The Count was an imposing figure of a man, over six feet tall and very much old world, but with a dash of the practical American intermingled with his historical background.

This was not surprising, since he had resided in California since 1927 and was an American citizen, married—a second marriage for him—to an American girl considerably his junior, with whom he lived at an impeccably decorated house in the Hollywood hills.

The house, which I only got to know after the Count's untimely death, is a far cry from the enormous expanse of the Steyersberg castle, but in its own way it was a perfect home for the two people who lived there happily for many years. For whatever the sinister aspects of the story, they had no powers under the warming rays of the California sun.

When we met, Degenhard von Wurmbrand was dressed conservatively—for California, anyway—in a gray business suit, but being Austrian, he was anything but stuffy. His conversation sparkled with wit and charm; his English of course was excellent, and we spent a pleasant hour together. Unfortunately I was under great pressure at the time from television work, so I could not come to his home on Bluebird Avenue.

He was 72 years old and, as a former Imperial officer, carried himself so erectly as to belie his years. Nothing about him gave a hint of illness or weakness, a point I find rather important in the light of later events.

It was his custom to visit his castle in the mountains of Austria every summer, to join his sister, the widowed Countess Kolowrat, in a few weeks of vacationing at a place that had been in their family for centuries. The Wurmbrand family goes back to the Middle Ages, and its members held high honors in the Austrian Empire.

After 1939, Degenhard did not return to his castle in the summer because of the war, and only his American ownership of the estate prevented the Russians from sacking it. His younger brother, Count Ernst, actually administered it until his death in 1960, while Degenhard continued a carefree existence in Hollywood. But there was always a shadow, an ever present threat that even the warmth of California could not dispel.

Degenhard von Wurmbrand—his full title was His Excellency, the Imperial Count of Wurmbrand-Stuppach—had grown up in the enormous castle, a gray building of some sixty rooms perched atop a tree-covered mountain some 49 miles south of Vienna, not terribly far from the busy Schwechat airport. He shared a room with his younger brother in the oldest wing of the castle, a wing going back well before the 17th century. Although Steyersberg has been completely modernized and has a bathroom for each bedroom, no structural changes whatever have changed its original appearance.

The room the two boys occupied, back at the turn of the

century, was a tower room looking onto the moat below and onto the distant rolling hills of Styria. It is in what is now the top floor of that wing, looming considerably above the surrounding landscape. I have looked out of that window at the corner of the room where you can see both eastward and southward, and the isolation, the feeling of remoteness, is intense. The room the boys shared was connected to another tower room by a dark corridor. Their sister Huberta occupied that other room. Underneath, the castle extended well into the rock.

Degenhard learned very early that the castle harbored a terrible secret. He was six years old and on his own, so to speak; his younger brother still had a nurse who shared the accommodations with the two children. The younger boy was two.

It was dark early one evening and nothing but blackness could be seen outside the windows. The nearest village was miles away and no lights broke the enveloping shadows. The nurse was reading a book—it was only about 7 P.M.—and the only light in the large room came from a small kerosene lamp on her night table. The younger boy was already asleep but Degenhard could not close his eyes. Somehow this night seemed different to him. Perhaps the budding sixth sense had already manifested itself at this early age, for Count Wurmbrand later became very psychic and was so to his end.

At any rate, the six-year-old was in bed, but fully awake, when his eyes happened to glance toward the corridor connecting the two rooms. Suddenly, he saw three black crows emerge from the corridor—flying into their room!

As the startled boy watched the strange birds which had seemingly come out of thin air, one of the crows alighted on the headboard of his brother's bed, while two perched on his bed. This was enough for him—instantly he pulled the blanket over his head. When he came up for air a moment later, there was no trace of the birds, and the nurse was reading quietly. She had not seen anything. Evidently the birds had meaning only for members of the Wurmbrand family!

When I visited Steyersberg Castle with my wife Catherine on September 6, 1965, Count Wurmbrand took me to that very room. Except for the soft carpeting now covering the floor and the up-to-date bathroom fixtures, it had not changed very much. The view from the windows was still breathtaking.

Again, it was dark outside, as the air was heavy with rain which had come down continuously all day. It was now four in the afternoon but the atmosphere was forbidding and depressing. The instant I set foot into that part of the castle, I felt myself pulled down and somehow found myself speaking in hushed tones. The Count suddenly looked very, very tired and old—quite different from the athletic Lord of the Manor who had greeted us at his gates earlier that day. Was the atmosphere of the room transforming him, too?

We discussed the past of the rock upon which the castle was built; originally erected in 1180, it passed into the Wurmbrand family in 1530 but it had fallen into disrepair when Degenhard's father rebuilt it. Degenhard himself added the bathrooms and other American touches, making it probably one of the best appointed old castles in the world.

Then our conversation turned to the ghostly crows.

"I have wondered all my life what it meant," the Count said. "I can see them even now!"

The specter of the crows—and other uncanny experiences, noises, footsteps where no one walked—troubled him through the years. But it was not until 1950 that he learned a little more about his predicament and what it meant.

"There was a German clairvoyant in California at the time," the Count explained, "and out of curiosity I went to see her. Immediately she drew back and asked me, 'What is this black entity I see behind you?' She thought I was *possessed.*"

"Possessed?" I said. Had a ghost left the castle and travelled all the way to Hollywood? Impossible. Ghosts stay put.

The clairvoyant wondered where the Count could have "picked up" this possessing force, and he could not think of any meaningful incident—except the appearance of the ghostly crows. The clairvoyant then made an appointment for Count Wurmbrand to see a Buddhist priest specializing in exorcising the possessed.

"Did it do any good?" I asked. The plot was becoming international.

"He did the ceremony three times," the Count recalled, "but after the first attempt I questioned him about the whole thing."

The Buddhist priest, who knew nothing whatever about the Count or his background, evidently was also a medium. He described three ragged men around the Count, men who protested their expulsion since they had some unfinished business.

The Buddhist priest asked that they explain themselves, and the restless spirits informed him that two ancestors of the Count's had done them wrong; having accused them falsely of treason, these earlier Wurmbrands had then tortured and killed the men in their castle. Even though this had happened a long time ago, the victims wanted revenge. They wanted the Count to kill, to commit a crime. That was their way of getting even for a wrong done in 1710!

Count Wurmbrand thought all this very strange, but then he recalled with terrifying suddenness how he had often felt an almost uncontrollable desire to kill, to commit murder—he, a normally gentle, peace-loving man.

Another thought struck him as he walked out of the Hollywood priest's house. All the phenomena of an uncanny nature had taken place in the room where he had seen the three crows—and that room was in a direct line above the dungeon. His father had ordered the ancient dungeon walled up, and it is inaccessible to this day; to get into it, one would have to break down a thick wall. If anyone had been tortured to death at Steyersberg Castle, it was at that spot.

Count Wurmbrand examined the historical records concerning his ancestors. In 1710 the castle belonged to a different branch of the family, and, oddly enough, two men shared ownership and command, for they were also generals in the Imperial army. Thus the ghosts' reference to two men having done them wrong made sense.

Nothing much happened to the Count in the subsequent years that would have reminded him of the ancient curse. But in 1961 he returned to Austria again and there he met a lady who had been a friend of his father and brother. She was the only person interested in psychic matters that the Count knew, outside of himself, and she therefore confided in him without reservation in such areas.

It appeared that a séance had been held at the castle in his absence, at which a then famed Vienna medium was present along with the lady and his brother. The man went into trance in one of the rooms of the castle. Suddenly, the electric lights dimmed quite by themselves for no apparent reason. Then they clearly heard heavy footfalls where nobody was seen walking. The lady had had enough and left the room, leaving the continuance of the séance to his brother.

After a while, Count Ernst also left and went to his room. But the invisible footsteps followed him right to his room. This so unnerved him that he asked the medium for further advice. The man offered to do his best, and, without having any foreknowledge of the events that had happened so many years ago in the boys' bedroom above the dungeon, went directly to that room although he could have gone to some fifty others.

"This is where I want to sleep," he explained, and so he did. The following morning he revealed that the ghost had communicated with him the night before. The ghost complained of having been wrongly imprisoned for treason and tortured by the two ancestor-generals. It was exactly the same story the Buddhist had told Count Wurmbrand in Hollywood—with one notable exception: here only one man claimed to have been wronged, only one ghost.

"Was that all?" I asked. It had been quite a story.

"Not entirely," Count Wurmbrand explained in a voice that

grew slowly more tired as night fell outside. "The curse included a provision for happiness. No Wurmbrand should have a happy marriage within these walls, the ghost claimed. And no Wurmbrand ever has."

I took some photographs in the haunted room, photographs that later showed remarkable superimpositions. Although my camera, double-exposure-proof due to a lock mechanism, cannot take anything but square pictures, I came up with a triple picture of oblong shape, showing areas of the room that were actually in back of me, areas the camera could not possibly have photographed under ordinary conditions—and there was no mirror or window to account for it. These pictures are now among my psychic photographs and I treasure them highly.

Another remarkable thing about them, however, was the way Count Wurmbrand looked in one of them. Very tired and ill, as if the shadows that were to come were already being etched on his face by supernormal means!

I did not want to strain my host, but there were some loose ends I wanted to clear up before we returned to the others. Because the Count's sister was not too keen on the subject, or so he felt—wrongly, as I later discovered—he and I had gone to the haunted room alone, leaving my wife to discuss music and art with Countess Juliana Wurmbrand, his wife, and Countess Kolowrat, the sister.

"Outside of yourself, your brother Ernst, and, of course, the medium, has anyone else experienced anything out of the ordinary in this castle?" I asked.

"During the years when I was in America, the lady I mentioned before who had brought the medium here once brought here a man who was not of the best character. He was a member of the Nazi party, so intentionally she put him into the haunted room. The next morning, he complained bitterly about it. There had been terrific noises all night and people 'trying to come in all the time.' Some force had tried to force itself into the room, he claimed."

Were there any records of the treason trial referred to by the ghost? We went down into the library of the castle, which was on the first floor and even nearer to the walled-up dungeon. It was an ill-lit, long room filled with manuscripts, some in a state of disorder and all covered with dust. A cursory examination yielded nothing of help.

"When was the last time you felt uneasy here?" I asked, finally.

"I wouldn't sleep in this room, I assure you," the Count answered. Earlier he had told me that the curse was still hanging over him and he had never really felt *safe* from it.

When he was at the castle, he simply avoided the areas he considered haunted and lived only in the other portions. There were the living and dining rooms, magnificent in their splendor and appointments, furnished as only a very old family can furnish their house. His own apartments were in one of the other wings, quite a walk from the big fireplace that graced the large dining room to which we now returned.

The day had been a long one, and one fraught with strange incidents. Somehow it felt like the script of a Hollywood horror movie, only we were not reading it—we were in it!

I had already—and foolishly—committed myself to leave Vienna in the morning, so I could not stay over. I promised to return the following summer with Sybil Leek, a medium, and finish off the ghost and the curse.

That, at least, was my intention, and I corresponded with the Wurmbrands on and off, until we could set a date to return.

Then, suddenly, there was silence. In December of 1965, I received a black-bordered letter bearing an Austrian postmark. Instinctively I knew what it meant before I opened it.

It was the official notification that my friend had passed away on November 17, and had been buried with all honors due him in the patron's church at nearby Kirchau, one of the villages "belonging" to the Steyersberg domain.

I was not satisfied with this formal announcement: I wanted

to know more. Had not my friend been in excellent health when we last saw him?

In June of 1966 I spent some time in Hollywood, and it was then that I finally saw the California home of the Wurmbrands. Countess Juliana brought me up to date on events.

Her husband had been taken ill with a minor complaint, but one sufficiently important to be looked after in a good hospital. There was no danger, nor was he indeed suffering very deeply. Several days went by and the Count became impatient, eager to return to active life again. Juliana visited him regularly, and if anything was wrong with my friend, it was his distaste at being in the hospital at all.

Then one night he had a small blood clot. Normally, a quick treatment is possible and the outcome need not be fatal. But that night, the doctor could somehow not be found in time, and precious moments ticked off. By the time help came, it was too late. Count Wurmbrand had died of an unrelated accident, an accident that need not have happened nor been fatal to him. Had the fingers of fate, the far-reaching rays of a grim curse finally reached their last victim?

For the Count died without direct male heir bearing his illustrious name, and so it is that the Steyersberg Castle is no longer in the hands of a Count Wurmbrand as I write this account of the strange curse that followed a man from Austria to sunny California, and back again to Austria. Who knows, if Degenhard von Wurmbrand had remained in California in 1965 he might still be alive.

I know this to be so, for I spoke to him briefly in the fall of 1964 when I passed through Hollywood. He was not sure at the time whether he could see us at his Castle in the summer of 1965 or not.

"Something tells me not to go," he said gravely.

"Then you should not," I advised. A man's intuition, especially when he is psychic and has had premonitions all his life as Wurmbrand had, should be heeded.

But the Count had business in Austria and in the end he relented and went, never to return to California. Thus it was that, before I could do anything about it, the Wurmbrand curse had found its mark.

THE TORMENTED TRAILER

Striptease artists usually stick to the world of flesh and blood but now
and again ghostly visitations do occur in their lives.

I received a communication (via the U.S. mail) from a comely young exotic dancer named Rita Atlanta.

Her initial letter merely requested that I help her get rid of her ghost. Such requests are not unusual, but what made her case unusual was the fact that her ghost appeared in a thirty-year-old trailer near Boston.

"When I told my husband that we had a ghost," she wrote, "he laughed and said, 'Why should a respectable ghost move into a trailer? We have hardly room in it ourselves with three kids.'"

It seemed the whole business had started during the summer when the specter made its first sudden appearance. Although her husband could not see what she saw, Miss Atlanta's pet skunk evidently didn't like it and moved into another room. Three months later, her husband passed away and Miss Atlanta was kept busy hopping the Atlantic (hence her stage name) in quest of nightclub work.

Ever since her first encounter with the figure of a man in her Massachusetts trailer, the dancer had kept the lights burning all night long.

Despite the lights, Miss Atlanta always felt a presence at the same time that her initial experience had taken place—between three and three-thirty in the morning. It would awaken her with such regularity that at last she decided to seek help.

At the time she contacted me, she was appearing nightly at the Imperial in Frankfurt, taking a bath onstage in an oversize champagne glass filled with under-quality champagne. The discriminating clientele that frequents the Imperial loved the French touch, and Rita Atlanta was, and is, a wow.

I discovered that her late husband was Colonel Frank Bane, an Air Force ace who had originally encouraged the Vienna-born girl to change from ballet to belly dancing, and eventually to what is termed "exotic" dancing, but which is better described as stripping.

I decided to talk to the "Champagne Bubble Girl" on my next overseas trip. She was working at that time in Stuttgart, but she came over to meet us at our Frankfurt Hotel, and my wife was immediately taken with her pleasant charm and lack of "show business" phoniness. Then it was discovered that Rita was a Libra, like my wife, Catherine, and we repaired for lunch to the terrace of a nearby restaurant to discuss the ups and downs of a hectic life in a champagne glass, not forgetting the three kids and a ghost in a house trailer.

In September of the previous year, she and her family had moved into a brand-new trailer in Peabody, Massachusetts. After her encounter with the ghost, Rita made some inquiries about the nice grassy spot where she had chosen to park the trailer. Nothing had ever stood on the spot before. No ghost stories. Nothing. Well . . . just one little thing.

One of the neighbors in the trailer camp, which is in Peabody, Massachusetts, came to see her one evening. By this time Rita's heart was already filled with fear, fear of the unknown that had suddenly come into her life here. She freely confided in her neighbor, a girl by the name of Birdie Gleason.

To her amazement, the neighbor nodded with understanding. She, too, had felt "something," an unseen presence in her house trailer next to Rita's.

"Sometimes I feel someone is touching me," she added.

"What exactly did *you* see?" I interjected, while the street noises of Frankfurt belied the terrifying subject we were discussing.

"I saw a big man, almost seven foot tall, about three hundred fifty pounds, and he wore a long coat and a big hat."

But the ghost didn't just stand there glaring at her. Sometimes he made himself comfortable on her kitchen counter, with his ghostly legs dangling down from it. He was as solid as a man of flesh and blood, except that she could not see his face clearly since it was in the darkness of early morning.

Later, when I visited the house trailer with my highly sensitive camera, I took some pictures in the areas indicated by Miss Atlanta: the bedroom, the door to it, and the kitchen counter. In all three areas, strange phenomena manifested on my film. Some mirrorlike transparencies developed in normally opaque areas, which could not and cannot be explained.

When it happened the first time, she raced for the light and turned the switch, her heart beating wildly. The yellowish light of the electric lamp bathed the bedroom in a nightmarish twilight. But the spook had vanished. There was no possible way a real intruder could have come and gone so fast. No way out, no way in. Rita had taken special care to double-lock the doors and secure all the windows. Nobody could have entered the trailer without making a great deal of noise. I have examined the locks and the windows—not even Houdini could have done it.

The ghost, having once established himself in Rita's bedroom, returned for additional visits—always in the early morning hours. Sometimes he appeared three times a week, sometimes even more often.

"He was staring in my direction all the time," Rita said with a slight Viennese accent, and one could see that the terror had never really left her eyes. Even three thousand miles away, the spectral stranger had a hold on the woman.

Was he perhaps looking for something? No, he didn't seem to be. In the kitchen, he either stood by the table or sat down on the counter. Ghosts don't need food—so why the kitchen?

"Did he ever take his hat off?" I wondered.

"No, never," she said and smiled. Imagine a ghost doffing his hat to the lady of the trailer!

What was particularly horrifying was the noiselessness of the apparition. She never heard any footfalls or rustling of his clothes as he silently passed by. There was no clearing of the throat as if he wanted to speak. Nothing. Just silent stares. When the visitations grew more frequent, Rita decided to leave the lights on all night. After that, she did not *see* him any more. But he was still there, at the usual hour, standing behind the bed, staring at her. She knew he was. She could almost feel the sting of his gaze.

One night she decided she had been paying huge light bills long enough. She hopped out of bed, turned the light switch to the off position and, as the room was plunged back into semi-darkness, she lay down in bed again. Within a few minutes her eyes had gotten accustomed to the dark. Her senses were on the alert, for she was not at all sure what she might see. Finally, she forced herself to turn her head in the direction of the door. Was her mind playing tricks on her? There, in the doorway, stood the ghost. As big and brooding as ever.

With a scream, she dove under the covers. When she came up, eternities later, the shadow was gone from the door.

The next evening, the lights were burning again in the trailer, and every night thereafter, until it was time for her to fly to Germany for her season's nightclub work. Then she closed up the trailer, sent her children to stay with friends, and left with the faint hope that on her return in the winter, the trailer might be free of its ghost. But she wasn't at all certain.

It was getting dark outside now, and I knew Miss Atlanta soon had to fly back to Stuttgart for her evening's work. It was obvious to me that this exotic dancer was a medium, as only the psychic can "see" apparitions.

I queried her about the past, and reluctantly she talked of her earlier years in Austria.

When she was a schoolgirl of eight, she suddenly felt herself compelled to draw a picture of a funeral. Her father was puzzled by the choice of so somber a subject by a little girl. But as she pointed out who the figures in her drawing were, ranging from her father to the more distant relatives, her father listened with lips tightly drawn. When the enumeration was over, he inquired in a voice of incredulity mixed with fear, "But who is being buried?"

"Mother," the little girl replied, without a moment's hesitation, and no more was said about it.

Three weeks later to the day, her mother was dead.

The war years were hard on the family. Her father, a postal employee, had a gift for playing the numbers, allegedly on advice from his deceased spouse. But Germany's invasion ended all that and eventually Rita found herself in the United States and married to an Air Force Colonel.

She had forgotten her psychic experiences of the past, when the ghost in the trailer brought them all back only too vividly. She was frankly scared, knowing her abilities to receive messages from the beyond. But who was this man?

I decided to visit Peabody with a medium to see what we could learn. I met Rita and she showed me around her trailer. It was a cold and moist afternoon.

Her oldest son greeted us at the door. He had seen nothing and neither believed nor disbelieved his mother. But he was willing to do some legwork for me to find out who the shadowy visitor might be.

It was thus that we learned that a few years ago a man had been run over by a car very close by. Had the dead man, confused about his status, sought refuge in the trailer—the nearest "house" in his path?

Was he trying to make contact with what he could sense was a medium, who would be able to receive his anxious pleas?

It was at this time that I took the unusual photographs of the areas Rita pointed out as being haunted. Several of these pictures show unusual mirrorlike areas, in which "something" must have been present in the atmosphere. But the ghost did not appear for me or, for that matter, Rita.

Perhaps our discovery of his "problem" and our long and passionate discussion of it had reached his spectral consciousness and he knew that he was out of his element in a trailer belonging to people not connected with his world.

Was this his way of finally, belatedly, doffing his hat to the lady of the house trailer, with an apology for his intrusions?

I haven't had any further word from Rita Atlanta, but the newspapers carry oversize ads now and then telling some city of the sensational performance of the girl in the champagne glass.

It is safe to assume that she can now bathe completely alone, something she had not been sure of in the privacy of her

Massachusetts trailer. For Rita, the eyes of a couple hundred visiting firemen in a Frankfurt nightclub are far less bothersome than one solitary pair of eyes staring from another world.

THE RESTLESS SEA CAPTAIN

When a New England salt has a grievance, he can sometimes take it to
his grave . . . that is, if he is headed *to* his grave. In this case, the sea
captain in question never really passed away completely. He is
still in what used to be his house, pushing people around
and generally frightening one and all.
Spending time in this house wasn't easy, but I did it, and somehow
survived the night. But I'm getting ahead of myself.

Some of the best leads regarding a good ghost story come to me as the result of my having appeared on one of many television or radio programs, usually discussing a book dealing with the subject matter for which I am best known—psychic phenomena of one kind or another. So it happened that one of my many appearances on the Bob Kennedy television show in Boston drew unusually heavy mail from throughout New England and even New York.

Now if there is one thing ghosts really don't care much about it is time—to them everything is suspended in a timeless dimension where the intensity of their suffering or problem remains forever constant and alive. After all, they are unable to let go of what it is that ties them to a specific location, otherwise they would not be what we so commonly (and perhaps a little callously) call ghosts. I am mentioning this as a way of explaining why, sometimes, I cannot respond as quickly as I would like to when someone among the living reports a case of a haunting that needs to be looked into. Reasons are mainly lack of time but more likely lack of funds to organize a team and go after the case. Still, by and large, I do manage to show up in time and usually resolve the situation.

Thus it happened that I received a letter dated August 4, 1966, sent to me via station WBZ-TV in Boston, from the owner of Cap'n Grey's Inn, located in Barnstable on Cape Cod. The owner, Mr. Lennart Svensson, had seen me on the show and asked me to get in touch.

"We have experienced many unusual happenings here. The building in which our restaurant and guest house is located was built in 1716 and was formerly a sea captain's residence," wrote Svensson.

I'm a sucker for sea captains haunting their old houses so I wrote back asking for details. Mr. Svensson replied a few weeks later, pleased to have aroused my interest. Both he and his wife had seen the apparition of a young woman, and their eldest son had also felt an unseen presence; guests in their rooms also mentioned unusual happenings. It appeared that when the house was first built the foundation had been meant as a fortification against Indian attacks. Rumor has it, Mr. Svensson informed me, that the late sea captain had been a slave trader and sold slaves on the premises.

Svensson and his wife, both of Swedish origin, had lived on the Cape in the early thirties, later moved back to Sweden, to return in 1947. After a stint working in various restaurants in New York, they acquired the inn on Cape Cod.

I decided a trip to the Cape was in order. I asked Sybil Leek to accompany me as the medium. Mr. Svensson explained that the Inn would close in October for the winter, but he, and perhaps other witnesses to the phenomena, could be seen even after that date, should I wish to come up then. But it was not until June 1967, the following year, that I finally managed to set a date for our visit. Unfortunately, he had since sold the inn and, as he put it, the new owner was not as interested in the ghost as he was, so there was no way for him to arrange for our visit now.

But Mr. Svensson did not realize how stubborn I can be when I want to do something. I never gave up on this case, and decided to wait a little and then approach the new owners. Before I could do so, however, the new owner saw fit to get in touch with me instead. He referred to the correspondence between Mr. Svensson and myself, and explained that at the time I had wanted to come up, he had been in the process of redoing the inn for its opening. That having taken place several weeks ago, it would appear that "we have experienced evidence of the spirit on several occasions, and I now feel we should look into this matter as soon as possible." He invited us to come on up whenever it was convenient, preferably yesterday.

The new owner turned out to be an attorney named Jack Furman of Hyannis, and a very personable man at that. When I wrote we would indeed be pleased to meet him, and the ghost or ghosts, as the case might be, he sent us all sorts of information regarding flights and offered to pick us up at the airport.

Mr. Furman was not shy in reporting his own experiences since he had taken over the house. He wrote:

> There has been on one occasion an umbrella mysteriously stuck into the stairwell in an open position. This was observed by my employee, Thaddeus B. Ozimek. On another occasion when the Inn was closed early, my manager returned to find the front door bolted from *the inside* which appeared strange since no one was in the building. At another time, my chef observed that the heating plant went off at 2:30, and the serviceman, whom I called the next day, found that a fuse was removed from the fuse box. At 2:30 in the morning, obviously, no one that we know of was up and around to do this. In addition, noises during the night have been heard by occupants of the Inn.

I suggested in my reply that our little team consisting, as it would, of medium (and writer) Sybil, Catherine (my wife at the time), and myself, should spend the night at the Inn as good ghost hunters do. I also requested that the former owner, Mr. Svensson, as well as any direct witnesses to phenomena, be present for further questioning. On the other hand, I delicately suggested that no one not concerned with the case should be present, keeping in mind some occasions where my investigations had been turned into entertainment by my hosts to amuse and astound neighbors and friends.

In the end it turned out to be best to come by car, as we had other projects to look into en route, such as Follins Pond, where we eventually discovered the possibility of a submerged Viking ship. The date for our visit was to be August 17, 1967—a year and two weeks after the case first came to my attention. But not much of a time lag, the way it is with ghosts.

When we arrived at the Inn, after a long and dusty journey, the sight that greeted us was well worth the trip. There, set back from a quiet country road amid tall, aged trees, sat an impeccable white colonial house, two stories high with an attic, nicely surrounded by a picket fence, and an old bronze and iron lamp at the corner. The windows all had their wooden shutters opened to the outside and the place presented such a picture of peace it was difficult to realize we had come here to confront a disturbance. The house was empty, as we soon realized, because the new owner had not yet allowed guests to return—considering what the problems were!

Quickly, we unburdened ourselves of our luggage, each taking a room upstairs, then returned to the front of the house to begin our usual inspection. Sybil now let go of her conscious self the more to immerse herself in the atmosphere and potential presences of the place.

"There is something in the bedroom . . . in the attic," Sybil said immediately as we climbed the winding stairs. "I thought just now someone was pushing my hair up from the back," she then added.

Mr. Furman had, of course, come along for the investigation. At this point we all saw a flash of light in the middle of the room. None of us was frightened by it, not even the lawyer who by now had taken the presence of the supernatural in his house in his stride.

We then proceeded downstairs again, with Sybil assuring us that whatever it was that perturbed her up in the attic did not seem to be present downstairs. With that we came to a locked door, a door that Mr. Furman assured us had not been opened in a long time. When we managed to get it open, it led us to the downstairs office or the room now used as such. Catherine, ever the alert artist and designer that she was, noticed that a door had been barred from the inside, almost as if someone had once been kept in that little room. Where did this particular door lead to, I asked Mr. Furman. It appeared it led to a narrow corridor and finally came out into the fireplace in the large main room.

"Someone told me if I ever dug up the fireplace," Mr. Furman intoned significantly, "I might find something."

What that something would be, was left to our imagination. Mr. Furman added that his informant had hinted at some sort of valuables, but Sybil immediately added, "bodies . . . you may find bodies."

She described, psychically, many people suffering in the house, and a secret way out of the house—possibly from the captain's slave trading days?

Like a doctor examining a patient, I then examined the walls both in the little room and the main room and found many hollow spots. A bookcase turned out to be a false front. Hidden passages seemed to suggest themselves. Quite obviously, Mr. Furman was not about to tear open the walls to find them. But Sybil was right: the house was honeycombed with areas not visible to the casual observer.

Sybil insisted we seat ourselves around the fireplace, and I insisted that the ghost, if any, should contact us there rather than our trying to chase the elusive phantom from room to room. "A way out of the house is very important," Sybil said, and I couldn't help visualizing the unfortunate slaves the good (or not so good) captain had held captive in this place way back.

But when nothing much happened, we went back to the office, where I discovered that the front portion of the wall seemed to block off another room beyond it, not accounted for when measuring the outside walls. When we managed to pry it open, we found a stairwell, narrow though it was, where apparently a flight of stairs had once been. I asked for a flashlight. Catherine shone it up the shaft: we found ourselves below a toilet in an upstairs bathroom! No ghost here.

We sat down again, and I invited the presence, whomever it was, to manifest. Immediately Sybil remarked she felt a young boy around the place, a hundred and fifty years ago. As she went more and more into a trance state, Sybil mentioned the name Chet . . . someone who wanted to be safe from an enemy . . . Carson . . .

"Let him speak," I said.

"Carson . . . 1858 . . ." Sybil replied, now almost totally entranced as I listened carefully for words coming from her in halting fashion.

"I will fight . . . Charles . . . the child is missing . . ."

"Whom will you fight? Who took the child?" I asked in return.

"Chicopee . . . child is dead."

"Whose house is this?"

"Fort . . ."

"Whose is it?"

"Carson . . ."

"Are you Carson?"

"Captain Carson."

"What regiment?"

"Belvedere . . . cavalry . . . 9th . . ."

"Where is the regiment stationed?"

There was no reply.

"Who commanded the regiment?" I insisted.

"Wainwright . . . Edward Wainwright . . . commander."

"How long have you been here?"

"Four years."

"Where were you born?"

"Montgomery . . . Massachusetts."

"How old are you now?"

There was no reply.

"Are you married?"

"My son . . . Tom . . . ten . . ."

"What year was he born in?"

"Forty . . . seven. . ."

"Your wife's name?"

"Gina . . ."

"What church do you go to?"

"I don't go."

"What church do you belong to?"

"She is . . . of Scottish background . . . Scottish kirk."

"Where is the kirk located?"

"Six miles . . ."

"What is the name of this village we are in now?"

"Chicopee . . ."

Further questioning gave us this information: that "the enemy" had taken his boy, and the enemy were the Iroquois. This was his fort and he was to defend it. I then began, as I usually do, when exorcism is called for, to speak of the passage of time and the need to realize that the entity communicating through the medium was aware of the true situation in this respect. Did Captain Carson realize that time had passed since the boy had disappeared?

"Oh yes," he replied. "Four years."

"No, a hundred and thirteen years," I replied.

Once again I established that he was Captain Carson, and there was a river nearby and Iroquois were the enemy. Was he aware that there were "others" here besides himself?

He did not understand this. Would he want me to help him find his son since they had both passed over and should be able to find each other there?

"I need permission . . . from Wainwright . . ."

As I often do in such cases, I pretended to speak for Wainwright and granted him the permission. A ghost, after all, is not a rational human being but an entity existing in a delusion where only emotions count.

"Are you now ready to look for your son?"

"I am ready."

"Then I will send a messenger to help you find him," I said, "but you must call out to your son . . . in a loud voice."

The need to reach out to a loved one is of cardinal importance in the release of a trapped spirit, commonly called a ghost.

"John Carson is dead . . . but not dead forever," he said in a faint voice.

"You lived here in 1858, but this in 1967," I reminded him.

"You are mad!"

"No, I'm not mad. Touch your forehead . . . you will see this is not the body you are accustomed to. We have lent you a body to communicate with us. But it is not yours."

Evidently touching a woman's head did jolt the entity from his beliefs. I decided to press on.

"Go from this house and join your loved ones who await you outside . . ."

A moment later Captain Carson had slipped away and a sleepy Sybil Leek opened her eyes.

I now turned to Mr. Furman, who had watched the proceedings with mounting fascination. Could he corroborate any of the information that had come to us through the entranced medium?

"This house was built on the foundations of an Indian fort," he confirmed, "to defend the settlers against the Indians."

"Were there any Indians here in 1858?"

"There are Indians here even now," Furman replied. "We have an Indian reservation at Mashpee, near here, and on Martha's Vineyard there is a tribal chief and quite a large Indian population."

He also confirmed having once seen a sign in the western part of Massachusetts that read "Montgomery"—the place Captain Carson had claimed as his birthplace. Also that a Wainwright family was known to have lived in an area not far from where we were now. However, Mr. Furman had no idea of any military personnel by that name.

"Sybil mentioned a river in connection with this house," Furman said. "And, yes, there is a river running through the house, it is still here."

Earlier Sybil had drawn a rough map of the house as it was in the past, from her psychic viewpoint, a house surrounded by a high fence. Mr. Furman pronounced the drawing amazingly accurate—especially as Sybil had not set foot on the property or known about it until our actual arrival.

"There was an Indian uprising in Massachusetts as late as the middle of the nineteenth century," Furman confirmed, giving more credence to the date, 1858, that had come through Sybil.

"My former secretary, Carole E. Howes, and her family occupied this house," Mr. Furman explained when I turned my attention to the manifestations themselves. "They operated this house as an inn twenty years ago, and often had unusual things happen here as she grew up, but it did not seem to bother them. Then the house passed into the hands of a Mrs. Nielson; then Mr. Svensson took over. But he did not speak of the phenomena until about a year and a half ago. The winter of 1965 he was shingling the roof, and he was just coming in from the roof on the second floor balcony on a cold day—he had left the window ajar and secured—when suddenly he heard the window sash come down. He turned around on the second floor platform and he saw the young girl, her hair windswept behind her. She was wearing white. He could not see anything below the waist, and he confronted her for a short period, but could not bring himself to talk—and she went away. His wife was in the kitchen sometime later, in the afternoon, when she felt the presence of someone in the room. She turned around and saw an older man dressed in black at the other end of the kitchen. She ran out of the kitchen and never went back in again.

"The accountant John Dillon's son was working in the kitchen one evening around ten. Now some of these heavy pots were hanging there on pegs from the ceiling. Young Dillon told his father two of them lifted themselves up from the ceiling, unhooked themselves from the pegs, and came down on the floor."

Did any guests staying at the Inn during Svensson's ownership complain of any unusual happenings?

"There was this young couple staying at what Mr. Svensson called the honeymoon suite," Mr. Furman replied. "At 6:30 in the morning, the couple heard three knocks at the door, three loud, distinct knocks, and when they opened the door, there was no one there. This sort of thing had happened before."

Another case involved a lone diner who complained to Svensson that "someone" was pushing him from his chair at the table in the dining room onto another chair, but since he did not see another person, how could this be? Svensson hastily had explained that the floor was a bit rickety and that was probably the cause.

Was the restless spirit of the captain satisfied with our coming? Did he and his son meet up in the Great Beyond? Whatever came of our visit, nothing further has been heard of any disturbances at Cap'n Grey's Inn in Barnstable.

THE SPECTRAL SUITOR

A troublesome ghost is often mistaken as coming from the Devil, while in truth people generally remain the same in character as a ghost as when they were living. Their frustration lies in the fact that their journey to the afterlife, whether it be Heaven or the next dimension of existence, cannot be completed until they let go of their earthly obsessions.

Mrs. G. wasn't one of those who were impressed by demonic outbursts and could not care less whether there was a devil or not. She had grown up in a well-to-do middle-class family and spent her adult years in the business world. At age nineteen, she met and married Mr. G. and they have had a happy life together ever since. There are no children, no problems, no difficulties whatever. She was always active in her husband's gasoline business, and only lately had she decided to slow down a little, and perhaps do other things, leisure time things, or just plain nothing when the mood would strike her.

At age forty-nine, she felt that it was just as well that she started to enjoy life a little more fully. Not that she was unhappy or frustrated in any way, but after thirty years of the gasoline business she longed for some fresh air.

One day in the spring of 1964, a friend suggested something new and different for them to do. She had read an advertisement in the local paper that had intrigued her. A Spiritualist church was inviting the general public to its message service. Why didn't they have a look?

"Spiritualist church?" Mrs. G. asked with some doubt. She really did not go for that sort of thing. And yet, way back in her early years, she had what are now called ESP experiences. When she talked to a person, she would frequently know what that person would answer before the words were actually spoken. It scared the young girl, but she refused to think about it. Her parents' home was a twelve-year-old house in a good section of Kansas City. It was just a pleasant house without any history whatever of either violence or unhappiness. And yet, frequently she would hear strange raps at night, raps that did not come from the pipes or other natural sources. Whenever she heard those noises she would simply turn to the wall and pretend she did not hear them, but in her heart she knew they were there.

Then one night she was awakened from deep sleep by the feeling of a presence in her room. She sat up in bed and looked out.

There, right in front of her bed, was the kneeling figure of a man with extremely dark eyes in a pale face. Around his head he wore a black and white band, and he was dressed in a toga-like garment with a sash, something from another time and place, she thought. She rubbed her eyes and looked again, but the apparition was gone.

Before long, she had accepted the phenomenon as simply a dream, but again she knew this was not so and she was merely accommodating her sense of logic. But who had the stranger been? Surely, the house was not haunted. Besides, she did not believe in ghosts.

As a young woman, she once heard a friend in real estate talk about selling a haunted house not far from them. She thought this extremely funny and kidded her friend about it often. Little did she know at the time how real this subject was yet to become in her later years!

The haunted house across the street was sold, incidentally, but nothing further was heard about it, so Mrs. G. assumed the new owners did not care or perhaps weren't aware of whatever it was that was haunting the premises.

Her own life had no room for such matters, and when her friend suggested they attend the Spiritualist church meeting, she took it more as a lark than a serious attempt to find out anything about the hereafter.

They went that next night, and found the meeting absorbing, if not exactly startling. Perhaps they had envisioned a Spiritualist meeting more like a séance with dark windows and dim lights and a circle of hand-holding believers, but they were not disappointed in the quality of the messages. Evidently, some of those present did receive proof of survival from dear departed ones, even though the two women did not. At least not to their satisfaction. But the sincere atmosphere pleased them and they decided to come back again on another occasion.

At the meeting they managed to overhear a conversation between two members.

"He came through to me on the Ouija board," one lady said, and the other nodded in understanding.

An Ouija board? That was a toy, of course. No serious-minded individual would take such a tool at face value. Mrs. G. had more time than ever on her hands and the idea of "playing around" with the Ouija board tickled her fancy. Consequently she bought a board the following week and decided she would try it whenever she had a moment all to herself.

That moment came a few days later, when she was all by herself in the house. She placed her fingers lightly on the indicator. This is a plastic arrow designed to point at individual letters and that way spell out entire words. Mrs. G. was positive that only her own muscle power could move the indicator but she was willing to be amused that afternoon and, so to speak, game for whatever might come through the board.

Imagine her surprise when the board began to throb the moment she had placed her hands upon it. It was a distinct, intense vibration, similar to the throbbing of an idling motor. As soon as she lifted her hands off the board, it stopped. When she replaced them, it began again after about a minute or two, as if it were building up energy again. She decided there was nothing very alarming in all this and that it was probably due to some natural cause, very likely energy drawn from her body.

After a moment, her hands began to move across the board. She assured herself that she was not pushing the indicator knowingly but there was no doubt she was being compelled to operate the indicator by some force outside herself!

Now her curiosity got the upper hand over whatever doubts she might have had at the beginning of the "experiment," and she allowed the indicator to rush across the board at an ever-increasing speed.

As the letters spelled out words she tried to remember them, and stopped from time to time to write down what had been spelled out on the board.

"Hello," it said, "this is John W."

She gasped and let the pencil drop. John W. was someone she knew well. She had not thought of him for many years and if his name was still imbedded in her unconscious mind, it had been dormant for so long and so deeply, she could scarcely accuse her own unconscious of conjuring him up now.

John W. had worshiped her before she was married. Unfortunately, she had not been able to return the feeling with the same intensity. Ultimately, they lost track of each other and in thirty years never saw each other again. She learned from mutual acquaintances, however, that he had also gotten married and settled down in a nice house not far from where she and Mr. G. lived. But despite this proximity, she never met him nor did she feel any reason to.

John W. was also in the gasoline business, so they did have that in common, but there had been difficulties between them that made a marriage undesirable from her point of view. He was a good man, all right, but not her "type," somehow, and she never regretted having turned him down, although she supposed he did not take it lightly at the time. But so many years had passed that time would have healed whatever wounds there might have been then.

When John W. died of heart failure in 1964, he was in his late fifties. Over the years he had developed a morbid personality and it had overshadowed his former gay self.

"Hello," the Ouija board communicator had said, "this is John W."

Could it be? she wondered. She put the board away in haste. Enough for now, she thought.

But then her curiosity made her try it again. As if by magic, the indicator flew over the board.

"I want to be with you, always," the board spelled out now. And then a very avalanche of words followed, all of them directed towards her and telling her how much he had always loved and wanted her.

Could this be something made up in her own unconscious

mind? Why would she subject herself to this incursion? For an incursion it soon turned out to be. Every day, practically, she found herself drawn to the Ouija board. For hours, she would listen to the alleged John W. tell her how much he wanted to stay with her, now that he had found her again.

This was punctuated with bitter complaints that she had hurt him, that she had not understood his great devotion for her.

As the weeks went by, her own personality changed and she began to take on more and more of his characteristic moods. Whereas she had been a light-hearted, gay person, she turned moody and morbid and her husband could not fail to notice the change that had come over his wife.

But she did not feel she could tell him what had happened, partly because she did not really believe it herself yet, and partly because she felt it might harm their marriage. So she pretended to be depressed and her husband understood, blaming her middle years for it.

By the winter of 1964, her life was no longer her own. In addition to the frequent Ouija board sessions, she now began to hear the man's voice *directly*.

"I am with you," he explained, fervently, and with her he was. There was never a moment where she could be sure he was not nearby. Her privacy was gone. She kept hearing his voice, sad, but nevertheless his voice as it had been in life, talking to her from somewhere outside, and yet seemingly inside her head at the same time. She could not understand any of this and she did not know how to cope with it at first.

She threw away the accursed Ouija board that had opened the floodgates to the invasion from the beyond. But it did not help much. He was there, always present, and he could communicate with her through her own psychic sense. She found it difficult to fall asleep. About that time she noticed she was no longer alone in bed. At first she thought it was her imagination, spurred on by fear, that made her *think* the undesired one was with her. But she soon felt his physical presence close to her body.

One night she extended her hand and clearly felt *something* other than air above her own body! She let out a scream and turned on the light. But this merely woke her husband and she had to explain it as a bad dream, so that he would not be alarmed.

Night after night, she felt John W.'s ethereal body next to or on top of hers. There was no mistake about it. He was trying to make love to her from the shadowy world he was in, something he had been denied while in the flesh. She fought off his advances as best she could, but it did not deter him in the least.

At the beginning of their communication with the board's help, she had still felt a kind of compassion for the poor devil who had died so sadly and rather early in his life. But whatever positive feelings she still harbored for him soon went by the board and her attitude turned into one of pure hate.

Nothing mattered in her life but to rid herself of this nightmare and return to the placid life she had been leading prior to the incident with the Ouija board.

John W. added threats and intimidation to his arsenal of evil now. Threats as to what he would do to her and her husband if she did not accept him willingly. Ultimately, she could not bear it any longer and decided to inform her husband of what she was going through.

At first she was fearful as to what he might say. Perhaps he would have her committed to an institution, or at best, subject her to the humiliating treatments of a private psychiatrist.

But her husband listened quietly and with compassion.

"Terrible," he finally commented, "we've got to get you out of this somehow."

She sighed with relief. He evidently believed her. She herself had moments now where she questioned her own sanity. Could such things be as the sexual invasion of a woman by a dead man? Was she not merely acting out her own suppressed desires due perhaps to middle-age change of life?

She went to seek the advice of a physician.

After a careful checkup, he found her physically sound but

suggested a psychiatric examination and possibly an EEG—an electroencephalogram—to determine brain damage, if any. None of these tests showed anything abnormal. After a while, she concluded that medicine men could not help her even if they should believe her story.

Meanwhile, the attacks became worse.

"You will always hear my voice," he promised her night and day. "You won't be able to get rid of me now."

She tried all sorts of things. Grabbing whatever books on the subject of possession she could find, she tried to learn whether others had suffered similar attacks. She tried her skill at automatic writing hoping that it might give the accursed ghost a chance to express himself and perhaps she might reason with him that way. But though she became a proficient automatist, it did not do any good.

The handwriting she wrote in was not hers. What she wrote down made no sense to her, but it was he who was using her in still one more way and so she stopped it.

That night, she felt him closer than ever. Suddenly she felt her heart being squeezed and she gasped for breath. For a few moments of agonizing fear, she felt herself dying of a heart attack. The next day she went to see her doctor again. Her heart was sound as could be. But she knew then that she had just relived the very moment of his death. He had died of just such a heart failure!

Clearly John W. was a disturbed personality in the in-between world in which he now existed. He could not distinguish right from wrong, nor indeed recognize his true status.

His hatred and love at once kept him glued to her body, and her environment, it would appear, unwilling and unable to break what must have been his strongest desire at the time of death.

During their courtship, he had appeared as a good person, unselfish and kind. Now he seemed bitter and full of selfish desire to own her, unwilling to let her go or do anything she asked him to.

She enlisted the help of a local amateur hypnotist, but he failed to put her under hypnosis. Discouraged, she lost all desire to live if it meant living on with this monstrous person inside her.

One day she saw a television program on which hypnotic treatment in parapsychological cases was the subject of discussion. Again encouraged, she asked for help and went to New York for an attempt to dislodge the unwanted entity from her body and soul.

This time she did go under, although not very deeply. But it was enough for the personality of John W. to emerge and carry on a conversation of sorts with the hypnotist.

"I want her to go with me, she is all I have now," he said, speaking through Mrs. G.'s mouth in trance.

Later she confirmed that she had been on the brink of suicide recently, and this had not been in a moment of panic but as if someone had actually made her attempt it. Luckily, she had managed to pull out of it just in time.

"Do you believe in a God?" the hypnotist asked.

"No," the entity replied and brushed the question aside. "I told her, she made life hell for me, now I'll make her life hell for her."

"But why do that?"

"No one wants me—I want to cry—you don't know what this is like—over here—nothing but darkness—"

Tears came down Mrs. G.'s cheeks now.

"It's me crying, not *her*," the voice of John W. said, and then, somewhat quieter, "No one wanted me as a child . . . I came from an orphanage . . . my grandparents never wanted me . . . she could have made me happy but she didn't want to. She's the only woman who would have made me happy, only her, but she doesn't want me."

"Then why force yourself on her? What is the point?"

"I force myself on her because I can make her miserable."

"You can't force love."

"I have no pride."

"Renounce her."

"I don't want to listen to you. She hates me now anyway. I'm going to take her with me . . . I'll get her, one way or another, I'll get her all right."

The hypnotist, patiently, explained about the freedom of the Other Side and how to get there by wishing to be with the loved ones who have preceded him.

"This is all new to me," the confused entity replied, but seemed for a moment to be thinking it over.

But it was only a brief squint at The Light, then darkness took over once again.

"I've made her cry . . . miserable . . . she made me miserable. I don't like the way she's lived her life. . . ."

Suddenly, the personality seemed to squirm as if from guilt.

Was this his own private hell he was in?

"I'm not really that person . . . I've been lying to her . . . just so I can be around her, I tell her one thing and then another. . . ."

"Then why not leave her and go on to the Other Side?"

"I want to but don't know how—I can't go without *her*."

The hypnotist tried again, explaining that other souls had been equally confused and been helped across the Great Divide.

The voice of the possessing entity hesitated. He was willing to go, but could he see Mrs. G. now and again? Visiting privileges, the hypnotist thought, with a bitter sense of humor.

"Will I be able to come back and see her?" the voice asked again.

But then the demented mind emerged triumphant.

"She hates me for what I've done to her. I'm not going to leave. I can do anything with her. Never could do it when living."

Now the hypnotist dropped the polite approach.

"You are to leave this woman," he intoned, "on pain of eternal damnation."

"I won't go."

"You will be in hell."

"She will be with me then."

"I send you away, the psychic door is closed. You cannot return."

"I will."

A moment later, Mrs. G. awoke, somewhat dumbfounded and tired, but otherwise no worse off than she had been when she had been put under by the hypnotist.

After she returned to Kansas City, she had some hopes that the power of John W. had been broken. But the molesting continued unabated. True, there had been conversation and the entity now knew at least that he was committing a moral offense. But evidently it did not matter to him, for the attacks continued.

After a while, Mrs. G. realized that her anxiety and abject fear were contributing factors to John W.'s unholy powers. She learned that negative emotions can create energies that become usable by entities such as John W. When she realized this fact, her attitude began to undergo a change.

Where she had been waiting for his attacks to occur and counting the moments when she was totally free from his possession, she now deliberately disregarded all he did and treated his presence with utter indifference. She could still feel the rage within him when he wanted to possess her, but the rage was slowly cooling. Gradually, her compassion for the bedeviled soul returned and as it did, his hold upon her weakened. He made his point, after all, and now the point no longer mattered. When last heard from, Mrs. G. was living quietly in Kansas City.

TERROR ON THE FARM

Often when people hear of a curse cast on a place or a house, they scoff or laugh it off as simple superstition. But for those who have lived with such traditions and legends, a curse is extremely difficult to ignore. Such was the case regarding an old farm house that had been in the Holler family for many generations. The last thing in the world that the Hollers wanted was a working curse, but that is exactly what happened, causing them worry and even sheer terror.

Enzersdorf on the river Fischa is a small hamlet of no great significance in the Austrian province of Lower Austria. The land around it is flat, the houses modest, and the streets dusty. Although the village is close enough to the capital for the more prosperous inhabitants to do their major shopping in Vienna, you get the feeling you're miles and miles from nowhere. That may be because this easternmost part of Austria had long been part of Hungary and the land had been owned by Hungarian noblemen, and their world is a quiet, slow-moving world in which modern progress has little significance. Some of the houses are very old and have stood here through Turkish occupations, French wars, and World Wars I and II, seemingly immune to the winds of change. One house in particular deserves notice: built of gray stone, of the kind that is quarried in the foothills of the Alps not too far away, it differs from the one-story farmhouses of the district in several ways. To begin with, it has a tile roof and very thick walls; only castles and fortresses have such walls in Austria. The outer wall encloses several buildings and the entire farmyard, thus making the house a world unto itself, as if it wanted to be safe from enemy attacks. Over the main gate, there is a coat of arms surmounted by an ecclesiastical design, for part of what is now an ordinary farmhouse was once a nunnery; although the name of it and the history of the order that built it are lost in antiquity. One family has owned the farmhouse for four centuries. Its ecclesiastical background goes back into the Middle Ages, one of the most turbulent periods in Austria's history.

The dusty road leading to the house is called the *Fischamenderstrasse*, the house bears the number 24, and despite its grimy gate, there is a surprisingly well-kept yard beyond. As one enters the grounds, a sturdy, one-story farmhouse stands on the left, which served as the Hollers' main living room. Next to it are the stables, followed by haylofts, another house, and the usual array of farm sheds and outbuildings which line the other side of the yard. Evidently the building to the right of the gate had been the nunnery. But the phenomena that had brought me here were all concentrated in the left wing of the farm.

In 1964 a Vienna newspaper had seen fit to write about my activities in an uninformed and snide manner. A young farmer by the name of Rudolf Holler, Jr., had read the article and written to me asking for my help. Austria is not a land that takes kindly to psychic research. Strongly influenced by materialistic thought and yet under the remnants of clerical domination, Austrians as a whole don't like to mention such things as ghosts or psychic phenomena for fear of being ridiculed. But this young man had a fine mind and his interests did include extrasensory perception. I was impressed by his plea and decided to go to Enzersdorf and see if I could break the ancient curse he felt was still operative at his ancestral farm.

Now curses are a strange thing. One's intellectual upbringing wants one to reject such a possibility, and yet the evidence exists that curses do work. For four centuries the Holler family had been plagued by seemingly inexplicable misfortunes in its affairs. The presence of a restless spirit had been felt by many who had visited there, and ghostly manifestations had occurred. Above all, the animals were never well, no matter how healthy they had been before they were brought to the Holler stables. As soon as they were part of their farm, they became weak and showed unmistakable signs of disease. Cows would no longer give milk; horses turned lame; and even pigs, the sturdiest of domestic animals, lay listless and depressed, despite excellent feed and treatment.

I was, of course, aware of ancient superstitions among farm folk concerning their livestock. Witchcraft accusations against innocent old women for an animal's illness fill the annals of European history from the Middle Ages to the eighteenth century.

But Mr. Holler did not point the finger at any living person. He rationalized the facts as he saw them, and came to the conclusion that a wrong had been done to someone in the past, and that this wrong had never been righted. Thus the curse continued to be operative.

Nobody had ever tried to do anything about these conditions. The stories of the curse had been told from father to son until young Rudolf first heard them as a child. But he was the first of the clan who knew what the word "parapsychology" meant. He was resolved to do something about the curse, and thus I found myself embarking on still another psychic adventure one summer day in 1965. Turhan Bey, my good friend and also a student of the occult, had offered to come along and drive my wife and me out to Enzersdorf.

We arrived in the late morning and immediately entered the farmhouse where Rudolf Holler and his family were already eagerly awaiting us. After I had looked around the place for a while, we settled down in the *gute Stube*, the good room, of the farmhouse and I asked Mr. Holler, the head of the family, to go over the problem with me.

"I myself have often heard knocks," he began, "always between 7:30 and 8 P.M. There was no natural explanation."

For twenty-seven years, ever since he came to this house, Holler had heard the knocks. To him it sounded as if someone were lifting up a plate and smashing it down again against a table.

But the most frightening of the unusual phenomena in the Holler farmhouse goes back even beyond that time. A few years before, Holler's sister-in-law Maria Sladek was seated in the very room we were in now. Suddenly she saw on old woman with long, unkempt hair appear in the room, walking by the bed. Without taking any notice of her, the woman walked out through the closed door at the other end of the room—a door leading to the stables. She walked with a distinct limp, supporting herself with a cane. Mrs. Sladek was frozen with fear. She knew there was no such person at the farm at the time and moreover, in a small hamlet, everybody is known. But she had never seen this woman before in her life.

At first, she tried to pass the whole incident off as imaginary.

But the stranger also appeared to an aunt and to a house guest who knew nothing whatever of the reputation of the farm as having a curse on it.

The curse showed itself in many other ways, as well. Holler had bought some of the finest cows in the district—cows that made him the envy of the area. But in a short while they turned ill and died.

"We tried to raise every kind of livestock in these stables," Holler explained, "not only cows, but chickens, pigs, goats. They all died quickly. There was something in that spot that made it impossible for them to be well."

I shook my head. Perhaps there was some underground radiation?

But the ghostly visitation seemed to point in a different direction. Holler went to consult the local church records for the past four hundred years. No sign of any violence or murder. If any crime had been committed here, it hadn't left any traces. But Holler, who had married into the family that had owned the farm for so long, did notice one unusual fact: the previous owners, all the way back, had all died at early ages, disease was rampant among them, and the land belonging to the farm, instead of expanding in the course of time, became smaller and smaller until it reached the very modest size of today's farm. Evidently the place had been unlucky for four hundred years. I questioned Holler about the woman who walked through the wall. What did she look like?

"An old woman wearing old-fashioned clothes," he explained, "hair hanging down. Not of this period."

Two years before our visit, while digging a cellar for an extension of the house, the Hollers came upon two human skeletons. The curious thing about these skeletons was an abundance of black spots in the area of the backbone, indicating that they had been poisoned. It seemed to the Hollers that things quieted down after the discovery of the bones, but they did not wish to test their luck too much. Instead they moved into the newer portion of the farm. As for the accursed stables, they have been empty ever since. No sense exposing good animals to bad vibrations.

When the bones were discovered, the family held a council. What to do with them? It was decided to take the matter to the local parish priest. The good father listened quietly as the story of the discovery was unfolded before him.

"Look," he said at last, "this is a most unusual matter, most unusual. What shall we do about it?"

"Why, that's obvious, Reverend Father," Holler replied, "bury them in holy ground."

"That's just it," the priest countered. "How is the ground to remain truly holy, when all sorts of strange skeletons are being buried in it, I ask you?"

Holler was somewhat taken aback.

"But, Father," he began, "after all, these are people. People deserve to be buried in the cemetery."

"I know, I know," the priest said impatiently, walking up and down in his study, "but you see, we've had a couple suicides here lately, and it's been giving us a bad name. And now you come with God knows what sort of people."

"God knows," Holler said quietly.

"I tell you what," the priest said finally, as if he had stumbled upon the philosopher's stone, "here is what you do."

"Bring them over to you?"

"No, no, Heaven forbid, don't do that. Where exactly are they now—I mean the bones?"

"Where we found them, in the ground, down in the cellar."

"Good," the man of the cloth nodded, "in that case, leave them there."

"Leave them there? But Reverend Father, the trouble we've been having—the ghost—"

The priest threw him a stern, forbidding glance. Holler wished he hadn't mentioned the word.

"Leave them there," the priest intoned again, "just close up the hole and forget it."

Holler wasn't enthused by this suggestion, but he could not very well bury the skeletons in the cemetery without official permission.

He took his leave and went back to the farm. Then, with the help of his sons, he quietly closed the shallow grave in the cellar and hoped that it would be all right with the skeletons.

Unfortunately the trouble continued.

I decided to question Holler's wife now. Her maiden name intrigued me. She was born Anna Toifel, meaning Devil. It was her family that had owned this very house for five hundred years, and the house itself was five hundred years old. Not many farmhouses are.

In 1925 her grandparents saw the ghostly woman walk into the room. They noticed that her long, unkempt hair was gray.

"Nothing we touched in this house ever worked out," she explained, "from the animals, who died on us, to lost money and bad crops. It seems as if something or someone wants us to get out of the place."

"Do you actually feel a presence?"

"*Ja*, sometimes I feel there is someone in back of me."

"And is there?"

"No. I feel it all the way from here to the little house in the rear where we sleep now. Someone is at the door, the doorknob moves, and there is never anyone there. But I clearly heard the doorknob move."

Finally I turned to Rudolf Holler, Jr., age twenty-five, who had originally contacted me in New York. He is a trained locksmith and works as a driver for his father. When he was small, he used to sleep in a crib in the back room. Rarely did he have a peaceful night. Bad dreams kept waking him up. Over the years, these nightmares kept getting worse. Only six months before our visit, he woke up from a deep sleep around midnight. The outside gate had been opened, and footsteps resounded outside. The footsteps came up to the porch in front of the house, up the stairs to the bedroom. Rudolf, fully awake by that time, sat up in bed waiting for someone to open the door to his room. The handle was pressed down, as if a hand were on it, and then there was silence. No sound of retreating footsteps. Finally he jumped out of bed and opened the door. He was quite alone. It was just after 1 A.M. He then realized that the ghostly visitation had taken a full hour to cross the distance from the garden gate to his bedroom door, a distance he would walk in less than two minutes.

He never saw the "old woman with the long, gray hair" while he was awake, but she kept appearing in his dreams at frequent intervals, exactly as she had been described by his family.

The bed stood over the spot where the skeletons had been found farther down. After the discovery of the bones, the restless nights ceased.

I noticed that another young man had joined our little group. It turned out to be Engelbert, age eighteen, the younger son of the Hollers.

"Not long ago I went to the movies in the village," Engelbert reported, "and my mind was completely absorbed by the picture I had seen. When I returned home in the dark and reached the garden gate, I suddenly became aware of a white figure standing near it. In a moment it was gone."

"What did it look like?"

"It was a luminous figure, thin and high—you couldn't make out any features or anything."

There matters stood at present, and the Hollers had the uneasy feeling that the curse was far from lifted. The bones were still not in hallowed ground. At first Mrs. Holler had objected to leaving them where they had been found, but with no viable alternative they had remained down there, and we decided to have a look at the spot.

There, barely visible in the murky semidarkness of the cellar, was nothing more than a stone slab in a cellar wall. Hardly a suitable grave. The Hollers had come with me and stood around now, waiting for some action. I did not have a medium with me so I had to try and get through to the restless ones myself. Turhan

Bey seemed depressed by the mere thought of the violence that had caused these unknown people's deaths.

Quickly I said a quiet prayer for them, asking them not to hold the present owners of the house responsible for whatever ancient wrongs might have been done to them.

Then we returned to the sunlight. It was about two o'clock by now and the Hollers brought out some country wine to share with us.

Afterwards, we toured the rest of the farm and then wished them good-bye.

On Easter of 1966, I heard again from Rudolf Holler, Jr. Things were still very tricky at the farm. The two boys had been standing in the entrance recently, working on a car. Rudolf was standing exactly above the spot where the two skeletons were still buried. The time was 2:30 P.M. and it was a quiet, chilly March day. Suddenly a strong gust of wind tore open the gate to the road, enveloped Rudolf in a blast of chilly air, and rushed on to close the inner gate with a loud bang. The two young men looked at each other in bewilderment. There had been no wind, no draft, nothing that could have caused so violent a reaction.

But shortly afterwards, one of their two valued geese, a breeding animal, became unaccountably ill and had to be killed.

Rudolf asked that I return to Enzersdorf with a trance medium, realizing that the restless ones had not yet found peace.

I have not heard further from the Hollers. Either they have adjusted to living in an accursed house, or the old lady with the cane has recognized her true status, perhaps stirred up by my ceremonial service at the "grave" of the two skeletons.

Were these her victims? Was she earthbound because of what she had done?

Poisoning of humans as well as animals was a favorite way of bringing destruction to one's enemies in the sixteenth century. Were we dealing here with a rural Lucrezia Borgia?

I can't help thinking that the skeletons should have been buried in the cemetery, for being buried close to a former nunnery isn't the same thing. Only the consecrated ground of a regular graveyard will do. That is, if you're a discriminating skeleton.

STRANGE BEDFELLOWS

One can never be quite sure who might drop in for a visit, but in all likelihood, the visitor would be of human dimension, and, for better or for worse, could be dealt with in some fashion.
But what about an unsuspecting, young woman who goes to bed only to find to her horror that she has an uninvited bedmate? And not just any intruder, but a *skeleton*!?

"My friend says this skeleton tried to get into bed with her," my friend Elizabeth Byrd said with conviction and looked at me straight, to see how I would react. I did not disappoint her. I shook my head with determination and informed her somewhat haughtily that skeletons do not get into people's beds, in fact, skeletons don't do much really except maybe on Halloween when kids dress up as them.

But Elizabeth is as good a researcher as she is an author— *Immortal Queen* and *Flowers of the Forest* are among her historical novels—and she insisted that this was not some sort of Halloween prank.

More to please her than out of curiosity, I decided to look into this weird tale. I never take stock in anything that I don't hear firsthand, so I called on Elizabeth's friend to hear all about this skeleton myself. I was prepared for a charming, talky, and garrulous spinster whose imagination was running away with her.

The name on the door read Dianne Nicholson, and it was one of those grimy walk-ups on New York's middle East Side that are slowly but surely turning into slums. Downstairs there was a gun shop and the house was one in a row of other nondescript houses. Children were playing in the street, and trucks lumbered by, creating a steady din that must have been unnerving to any resident of this building. All in all, it was, without question, what New Yorkers call a "neighborhood."

I pressed the bell and, when the buzzer responded, walked up a flight of stairs where I found the door to the apartment slightly ajar.

I stepped inside and closed the door behind me.

"Miss Nicholson?" I said tentatively.

"Coming," said a bell-like young voice from the back of the dimly-lit apartment.

As my eyes got used to the place I distinguished that it consisted of a longish foyer, from which doors led to a kitchen, another room, and a small room, reading right to left. It was full of furniture and things and a glance into the small room on my left showed stacks of papers, a drawing board, and other graphic art paraphernalia strewn about.

My investigation was interrupted by the arrival of Miss Nicholson. It was immediately clear that my image of her had been wrong. An ash blonde of perhaps twenty-two or three, she was slight and erect and looked very determined as she greeted me.

"I'm so glad you came," she began and led me to the couch along the wall of the foyer. "This thing has been getting out of hand lately."

I held up my hand, for I did not want to lose a word of her account. Within a minute, my tape recorder was purring away and the story unfolded.

Dianne Nicholson came to New York from her native Atlanta in the middle of 1964. By training she was a writer, or more specifically, a writer of publicity, advertising, and promotional material, and she was presently working with an advertising agency in Manhattan. She was much too busy with the first task of looking for a job, and then of maintaining it, to pay much attention to the house and the little apartment in it that she had rented.

The apartment was inexpensive, within her budget, so she did not have to share it with a roommate, and the building was also convenient to her place of work.

In addition, she did a lot of extra work at home, free-lance accounts, to better her income, so she was rather absorbed in her professional activities most of the time, seldom allowing herself the luxury of aimless dreaming. Her social life was pleasant, but underneath it all ran a very practical streak, for Dianne had come to New York to make good as a career girl, and work was her way of getting there.

She knew few if any of her neighbors, most of whom were not in her social or professional strata to begin with. But she did manage to strike up a friendship with the girl who had an apartment a few stories above hers. This was a rather buxom German girl in her early thirties who went by the single name of Karina. An artist specializing in small drawings, cards, and other objects on the borderline between art and craft, Karina went around her place most of the time wearing miniskirts when miniskirts had not yet been invented. Her life was lived mainly by herself and she was happy to pursue this kind of career. Evidently she had left behind her in Germany a far different life, but there were no regrets. The two girls visited each other frequently, and it made both of them feel safe to know either one of them was not entirely alone in this dank building.

It was the middle of 1965, after living in the building for about a year, that Dianne became alarmed by a sequence of events she could not cope with.

At the time, she slept in the smaller room, off the foyer, which later became her workroom.

She awoke there one night and saw a figure standing at her door. It was a rather tall woman, wearing what to Dianne looked like a long nightgown. The figure also wore a kind of Mother Hubbard cap, like a granny would—and yet, Dianne quickly realized that this was not an old figure at all.

As Dianne, with curiosity at first, and increasing terror later, sat up in bed and studied the apparition, she noticed that the figure was luminescent and emitted a soft, white glow. The face, or rather the area where the facial characteristics should be, was also aglow, but she could not make out any features. As yet unsure as to what the figure was, Dianne noticed she could not distinguish any hands either.

At this moment the figure left the spot at the door and got into bed with her.

Dianne's first impression, when the figure got close, was that of a skeleton, but when it got into bed with her she realized that it was more of a waxen figure, very cold but as hard as flesh would be.

Her thoughts racing through her mind while practically paralyzed by the whole thing, Dianne tried to reason it out. Then she said to herself, why, it must be my mother. What in the world would come into bed with her?

Later, she realized that it wasn't her mother, of course. But at the moment she preferred to think so, recalling how her mother had often crawled into bed with her when she was a child. And yet she knew at this moment, crystal clear, that the white figure next to her was that of a young woman.

Touching the figure, she felt hard substance underneath the gown.

"I must see your face," she mumbled and tried to see the stranger's face. But the figure acted as if she were asleep and did not wish to be disturbed.

Dianne reached out and pulled the covers off the bed. She found herself staring into a mirror. Now she realized why she had not been able to see the creature's hands before. They weren't really hands at all, but were more like a skeleton's bony fingers, holding up a mirror in front of the figure's face.

Then the mirror moved and disclosed what took the place of a face: a glowing white round in which neither eyes, nose, nor teeth could be distinguished and yet the whole figure was more than a mere anatomical skeleton—it was a roughly covered skeleton figure—more than mere bones and not quite flesh and skin, but somewhere in between.

Dianne's normal reactions finally caught up with her: she found herself sinking into a slow state of shock at what she had discovered. At this moment, the figure disappeared. Not by retreating to the doorway from where it had come, but just by dissolving into the bed itself.

Dianne leaped out of bed, threw on a robe and raced upstairs to her friend's apartment. For days after, she trembled at the thought of the unspeakable one returning, and she tried hard to convince herself that she had dreamed the whole incident. But in her heart she knew she had not.

From that day on, however, she became increasingly aware of a human presence other than her own in the apartment. More from self-preservation through knowledge than from idle curiosity she bought some books dealing with psychic phenomena.

Early in December this oppressive feeling became suddenly very strong. She had moved her bed into the other bedroom, with a wall separating the two areas. One night she *knew* that an attack had been made upon her and that the evil personality involved was male. She slept with all the lights on from that moment. With mounting terror she would not go off to sleep until daylight reassured her that no further dangers were about.

Then, in early January, just before I came to see her, Dianne had another visit from a white, luminous figure. It was evening, and Dianne had just gotten to sleep. Suddenly she awoke, prodded by some inborn warning system, and there, in the entrance to her present bedroom, stood a vague, smoke-like figure of some luminescence. After a moment it was gone, only to return again later that same night. What did the figure want of her? This was not the skeletal visitor from before but definitely a masculine personality.

Dianne knew this entity was after her, and wanted to take her over. On one occasion in December she had felt him take over her nervous system, as she sat helplessly on her bed. Her muscles went into spasm as if they were no longer under her conscious control. Desperately she fought the invader, trying to keep her thoughts on an even keel, and ultimately she won out. The strange feeling left her body and she was able to relax at last.

Extrasensory experiences had plagued Dianne since childhood. When she was fourteen and going to high school, a close friend and sorority sister wrote to her with a strange request. Would she sing at her funeral? Now Dianne had been singing in choir and her friend knew this. But there was no logical reason for so strange a request from a fifteen-year-old girl. Three days after receiving the letter Dianne had a strange dream, in which she saw her friend in front of a large crowd, with her arms wide open, and calling out to Dianne, "Please help me!"

At this point, the dream faded out. She woke up after the dream and noticed that the clock showed 12:45 A.M., Friday.

Sunday night, the identical dream returned, only this time it ended abruptly rather than gently fading out. She discussed the dreams with her classmates in school but could not puzzle out the meaning. On Tuesday she received a phone call from her mother, informing her that her friend had been in an automobile accident on Friday, and, at the time of Dianne's first dream, her friend had just gone under anesthetic at the hospital. At the time of the second dream, which ended abruptly, the girl died.

There were other instances of premonitions come true, of feelings about events that later transpired—making Dianne aware of the fact that she had something special, yet in no way intruding on her practical approach to life.

When she first moved into her present apartment, she found that most of the buildings in the area were occupied by people on welfare relief. But the house she moved into had recently been renovated, making it suitable for higher-rent tenants, as had two others nearby, giving hope that the entire neighborhood might eventually adopt a different image.

Although one of Dianne's boyfriends, a photographer, felt nothing special about the apartment, two of her female friends did. There was Karina, the artist upstairs, for instance. She would not stay long, complaining the place gave her the creeps. Elizabeth Byrd also felt an oppressiveness not borne out by the decor or furniture of the place, for Dianne had managed to make the place comfortable and pleasant as far as the purely physical aspects were concerned.

After a while she quit her Madison Avenue job and became a free-lancer. This necessitated her spending much more time at home. In the daytime, she found the place peaceful and quiet and she managed to get her work done without trouble.

But as soon as the shadows of night crept over the horizon, fear began to return to her heart. The fear was not borne from darkness or from the presence of the unknown; it was almost a physical thing with her, something very tangible that seemed to fill a space within the walls of her apartment.

Dianne thought herself safe from the specter in the daytime until one morning she was awakened by a strange noise. She had gone to bed late after putting in long hours of work, and slept until 10 A.M. The noise, she soon realized, was caused by a wooden coat hanger banging heavily against the bedroom door. Still half-asleep, Dianne assured herself that the draft was causing it. She got out of bed, fully awake now, and walked toward the door. The noise stopped abruptly. She checked the door and windows and found everything closed. There could not have been a draft. Still unconvinced, she huffed and puffed to see if her breath would move the hanger. It didn't.

She began to have some strange dreams, several similar ones in succession. In these dreams the skeleton-faced white woman appeared to her and wanted to take her with her.

As the weeks rolled by, more and more strange incidents tried her patience sorely. There was the time she had gone to sleep with all lights burning, when she saw an explosion of light in the living room. It was not hallucinatory, for she saw it reflected in the dark tube of her television set. Another time she was in the bedroom when she heard the sound of glass breaking in the living room. The lights in the living room and the kitchen went out at the same moment. She entered the living room, expecting to see the remnants of a bulb that might have blown up, but there was nothing on the floor. The light switches, however, in both living room and kitchen had been switched off by unseen hands. At this moment her friend Karina came down from upstairs and Dianne was never so glad in her life to see a friendly human face.

Since Dianne Nicholson had gotten to be quite frantic about all this I decided to arrange for a séance to get to the bottom of the disturbances with the help of a good medium. We agreed on June 17, 1966, as the date, Sybil Leek was to be my medium, and Theo Wilson, a reporter from the *Daily News*, would come along to witness and report on the investigation.

Meanwhile, Karina had also had her share of run-ins with uninvited guests. Her apartment is on the fifth floor. One day

Karina was standing in front of her mirror when she noticed a ghostly figure—or rather a glowing outline. At the same time she felt a strong urge to cut her hair short and be like the apparition. She felt the ghostly presence wanted to possess her or express itself through her and she became frightened. A little later she was down on the second floor with Dianne, when both girls heard a sharp banging noise, as if someone had dumped a heavy object on the floor next to the entrance of the apartment. Their first impression was that a package had been delivered and they rushed to see what it was. But there was nothing there.

When the seventeenth of June arrived it turned out to be one of those oppressive, prematurely hot nights New York is famous for, or rather infamous for, but the date had been set and everyone was ready. I also brought along a motion picture camera and, on arrival, had deposited Sybil with Karina so that I might discuss the events leading up to the investigation once more for the benefit of Theo Wilson of the *News*. Naturally Sybil was not to hear any of this nor was Karina allowed to discuss anything with her temporary guest but the weather—at the moment a most timely subject.

Half an hour later I brought Sybil inside the second floor apartment. Did she feel anything here clairvoyantly?

"You'll probably laugh at this," Sybil said, "but I have a tremendous feeling about horses."

I didn't laugh, and even though I knew of Sybil's love for and interest in domestic animals, I noted the statement for later verification.

"What about people, though?" I pressed. A heavy oak chair had been placed near the entrance to the smaller room where Dianne had experienced the skeletal intruder originally. The chair was meant for Sybil to sit in and faced away from the small room.

"Behind this chair," Sybil now said, "there is a touch of coldness . . . some nonphysical being, definitely."

The feeling was only fleeting, her main sensation being of a country place with horses, and then that touch of "someone."

I decided to place Sybil into trance now and we—our hostess Dianne Nicholson, a gentleman friend of hers, Karina, Theo Wilson, and myself—grouped ourselves around her. Sybil took the chair facing away from the little room.

After a few moments, heavy, labored breathing replaced the measured breath of Sybil's normal personality. Words came across her lips that I could not yet make out, gradually becoming louder and firmer. I kept asking for a name—asking that the presence identify itself. Eventually the name was clear.

"Jeremy Waters," Sybil had said.

"Speak louder," I commanded.

"Go away," the voice countered, and added, "Jeremy."

"Why should Jeremy go away?"

"Why did he do it . . . nice stock . . . I'm hurt . . . Jeremy, Jeremy Waters . . ."

"Who are you?"

"Waters."

"Who is Jeremy?"

"Jeremy Waters, my son . . . I'll find him . . . ran away . . . left me . . . what'd he leave me for? . . . Mary Collins . . ."

It dawned on me now that Jeremy Waters, Sr., was complaining about Jeremy Waters, Jr.

"Is this your house?" I asked.

"House? There is not a house," the voice came back, somewhat astonished.

"Store place . . . I work here . . . waiting for Jeremy . . . where did they go, Jeremy and Maria . . . his woman . . ."

"How long ago was this?"

"Strange . . . fifty-four . . . where's everyone?"

"Tell me about yourself so I can help you."

"I don't trust you. What have you done with him?"

"What sort of work does he do?"

"A boat. He brings things here."

"When were you born?"

"Twenty-two."

"Where?"

"Hudson village . . ."

"What is your wife's name?"

"Margie."

"Where was she born?"

"Far . . . in Holland."

"Any children?"

"Jeremy . . . three."

When I asked what church he belonged to I got a disdainful snort in reply.

"Churches . . . churches . . . I do not go."

"What sort of place is this?"

"What do you come here for? Fall on your knees . . ." he said, instead, and added, "Find Jeremy . . . he should repent his sins . . . honor thy father and thy mother . . . where am I? There are too many people . . ." The voice sounded confused and worried now.

"And where's his clothes?" he demanded to know.

I started to explain the passage of time.

"Repent, repent," he mumbled, instead, barely listening.

"Why did they do it? Hurt me?"

"Who is this woman you mentioned?"

"Maria Goulando." It had sounded like Mary Collins to me at first, but now there was no mistaking the odd name. "She is Jeremy's woman."

"Is he married to her?"

"It is wrong to marry a Catholic," the voice said sternly.

"Is the girl a Catholic?"

"Yes."

"Did he marry her?"

"Over my dead body."

"He didn't marry her then?"

"No . . . the church won."

"Where is the woman now?"

"With Jeremy."

"If you find them, what will you do?"

"Make him repent."

This was said with so much bitterness I decided to take another tack with my questioning. "Have you hurt anyone, Jeremy?" I said.

"Why are you asking me . . . I'm not going to talk," he shot back, defiant again.

"Do you know where you are?"

"Outside the church."

"What church?"

"Lutheran church."

"Are you a Lutheran then?"

"Was . . ."

"What are you now?"

"*Nothing* . . ."

"What street is the church on?"

"Vall Street."

If he meant to say Wall Street he said it with a strange inflection. I asked him to spell it.

Puzzled and haltingly he said, "Veh—ah—el—el," spelling the W the way a European might spell it, especially a Dutchman or German.

"Wall Street," the voice said more clearly now, this time pronouncing it correctly.

"Name of the church?" I inquired.

"Why—can't—I—find—him?" it came back haltingly.

"What is this place used for?"

"Store things in the back . . ."

"Where do you live?"

"Hudson . . . up the Hudson."

Again I asked for the year he thought we were in.

"Fifty-four . . ."

This is where I made a mistake, perhaps.

"Eighteen fifty-four?" I said. I never like to lead.

"Yes," the voice acknowledged and added, "February . . .

today the fifteenth . . ."

"How old are you?" I asked.

"Today is my birthday."

"And your son is not with you?"

"Yes . . . ingratitude shall be his ruin."

"Did you kill anyone?"

"Go away, go away . . ." The voice sounded angry now as if I had hit on a sensitive topic. I reasoned with him, explaining about the passage of time.

"Your son has long died," I explained.

He would not accept this.

"You're a foreigner," he suddenly said, "what do you want? *She's* a foreigner."

"You don't like foreigners?"

"No."

"Did you kill Maria?"

"She was a foreigner," he said with contempt in his voice.

I asked him to make a clean breast of his guilt feelings so that he might free himself from the place we had found him. There was a long, long pause. Finally he understood and listened quietly as I sent him away to rejoin his dead son. Soon after, I recalled Sybil to her own body. None the worse for her experience, she remembered absolutely nothing that had transpired during the séance.

So there were two ghosts, Jeremy Waters and the girl Maria.

My next step was to check out the names given and see how they connected with the place we were in.

Naturally I assumed that 1854 was the period I should check, since the ghost had acknowledged that date. But there was nothing in the records indicating a Jeremy Waters at that date living on 21st Street.

The only clue of some interest was the name of one James Waters, a "carman" who lived on East 22nd Street between Second and Third Avenues as of 1847, according to Doggett's *New York Directory* for that year. But the thought did not leave me that the "18" was added to the ghost's "54" by my suggestion. Could he have meant 1754?

I decided to check that earlier date. Suddenly things became more interesting.

The entire piece of land on which this and other houses in the block were standing had originally belonged to the Watts family. The Watts city residence stood at 59 East Twenty-first Street and John Watts, Sr., owned the land in 1754, together with his son, John Watts, Jr. I was struck by the similarity of names of father and son, a parallel to Jeremy, Sr., and Jeremy, Jr. They had acquired the land in 1747 from James De Lancey, the elder Watts' brother-in-law. It was then a farm of 130 acres and extended from Twenty-first Street to the East River. Spooner's *Historical Families in America*, which gives these and other details of the prominent Watts family, also states briefly that a third John Watts was born to the young John in 1775, but died unmarried.

I was still struggling with the research on this case, when Theo Wilson's piece on our séance appeared in the New York *Daily News*. Theo was impressed by the sincerity of both approach and method and reported the investigation factually.

Because of her article a gentleman named Charles Burhaus contacted me with additional information on the Watts family; his father's sister had been married to the last of the Wattses. The Wattses did indeed come from the Hudson Valley and most of them are buried at Tivoli, New York.

The Wattses were very religious and fervent Protestants. "Old John Watts," Mr. Burhaus reports, "disapproved of his son's way of living."

When Mr. Burhaus's grandmother invited his Aunt Minnie to stay at the ancestral Watts house in Tivoli—Mr. Burhaus was then but a child—the lady refused to stay, explaining that the house was haunted by a ghost who liked women.

If there was a storehouse with boats nearby, as the ghost had claimed, on what is now East Twenty-first Street, 1854 would not fit, but 1754 would.

Jeremy Waters and John Watts are not identical names but I have encountered ghost personalities who, for reasons of honor, have disguised their true identities until the skill of the investigator was able to uncover their cover.

So much of the Waters father-and-son relationship seems to fit the Watts father-and-son relationship, the place is correct, and the first names are identical for father and son in both instances, that I cannot help feeling that we have this kind of situation here. If the son ran away with an unacceptable woman, the father would naturally not wish to divulge to a stranger, like me, his true identity, yet he might talk about the events themselves, being emotionally bound to them still.

Miss Nicholson had no further troubles in the apartment after that. She also moved a few weeks later and the new occupants, if they know of my investigation at all, have not seen fit to complain about any disturbance.

I can only assume that both Jeremy Waters, Sr., and the hapless girl he hurt have found their way across the boundary of the spirit world, which in any event is much nicer than a rooming house on East Twenty-first Street.

One more item gave me food for thought. I had taken a number of still photographs during the two visits to the apartment. When they were developed, several of them showed white shadows and streaks of light that could not be accounted for by natural explanations.

I mailed a set to Dianne Nicholson via first-class mail. It never reached her. A letter, containing some data on the apartment and its past, which she had mailed to me about the same time, never reached me. When I brought the negatives of my pictures to have another set of enlargements made, the lab lost the negatives or rather could not account for them, no reason given.

Finally we had to rephotograph the only existing set of prints to make duplicates.

Coincidence? Perhaps.

If there is such a thing.

AMERICA'S MOST HAUNTED

It is rare that a haunting can be observed by so many, so often, and in
such horrifying detail as in the case of San Diego's Whaley House.
Now a celebrated museum and landmark, the Whaley House caters to
scores of tourists, while its spiritual visitors continue to frequent the
historical site. The curators have kept an exact record of
the house's hauntings, both past and present.
Anyone who doubts the actuality of ghosts need only
spend a night at the Whaley House.

I first heard about the ghosts at San Diego's Whaley House through an article in *Cosmic Star*, Merle Gould's psychic newspaper, back in 1963. The account was not too specific about the people who had experienced something unusual at the house, but it did mention mysterious footsteps, cold drafts, unseen presences staring over one's shoulder and the scent of perfume where no such odor could logically be—in short, the gamut of uncanny phenomena. My appetite was whetted. Evidently the curators, Mr. and Mrs. James Reading, were making some alterations in the building when the haunting began.

I marked the case as a possibility when in the area, and turned to other matters. Then fate took a hand in bringing me closer to San Diego.

I had appeared on Regis Philbin's network television show and a close friendship had developed between us. When Regis moved to San Diego and started his own program there, he asked me to be his guest.

We had already talked of a house he knew in San Diego that he wanted me to investigate with him; it turned out to be the same Whaley House. Finally we agreed on June 25th as the night we would go to the haunted house and film a trance session with Sybil Leek, then talk about it the following day on Regis's show.

Sybil came over from England a few years ago, after a successful career as a producer and writer of television documentaries and the author of a number of books on animal life and antiques. At one time she ran an antique shop in her beloved New Forest area of southern England. Her name came to the attention of Americans primarily because of her religious convictions: she happened to be a witch. Not a Halloween type witch, to be sure, but a follower of the Old Religion, the pre-Christian Druidic cult which is still being practiced in many parts of the world. Her personal involvement with witchcraft was of less interest to me than her great abilities as a trance medium. I tested her and found her capable of total dissociation of personality, which is the necessary requirement for good trance work. She can get "out of her own body" under my prodding, and lend it to whatever personality might be present in the atmosphere of our quest. Afterwards, she will remember nothing and merely continue pleasantly where we left off in conversation prior to trance—even if it is two hours later! Sybil lends her ESP powers exclusively to my research and confines her "normal" activities to a career in writing and business.

We arrived in sunny San Diego ahead of Regis, and spent the day loafing at the Half Moon Inn, a romantic luxury motel on a peninsula stretching out into San Diego harbor. Regis could not have picked a better place for us—it was almost like being in Hawaii. We dined with Kay Sterner, president and chief sensitive of the local California Parapsychology Foundation, a charming and knowledgeable woman who had been to the haunted Whaley House, but of course she did not talk about it in Sybil's presence. In deference to my policy, she waited until Sybil left us. Then she told me of her forays into Whaley House, where she had felt several presences. I thanked her and decided to do my own investigating from scratch.

My first step was to contact June Reading, who was not only the director of the house but also its historian. She asked me to treat confidentially whatever I might find in the house through psychic means. This I could not promise, but I offered to treat the material with respect and without undue sensationalism, and I trust I have not disappointed Mrs. Reading too much. My readers are entitled to all the facts as I find them.

Mrs. Reading herself is the author of a booklet about the historic house, and a brief summary of its development also appears in a brochure given to visitors, who keep coming all week long from every part of the country. I quote from the brochure.

The Whaley House, in the heart of Old Town, San Diego— restored, refurnished and opened for public viewing—represents one of the finest examples extant of early California buildings.

Original construction of the two-story mansion was begun

on May 6, 1856, by Thomas Whaley, San Diego pioneer. The building was completed on May 10, 1857. Bricks used in the structure came from a clay-bed and kiln—the first brick-yard in San Diego—which Thomas Whaley established 300 yards to the southwest of his projected home.

Much of "Old San Diego's" social life centered around this impressive home. Later the house was used as a theater for a traveling company, "The Tanner Troupe," and at one time served as the San Diego County Court House.

The Whaley House was erected on what is now the corner of San Diego Avenue and Harney Street, on a 150-by-217-foot lot, which was part of an 8½-acre parcel purchased by Whaley on September 25, 1855. The North room originally was a granary without flooring, but was remodeled when it became the County Court House on August 12, 1869.

Downstairs rooms include a tastefully furnished parlor, a music room, a library and the annex, which served as the County Court House. There are four bedrooms upstairs, two of which were leased to "The Tanner Troupe" for theatricals.

Perhaps the most significant historical event involving the Whaley House was the surreptitious transfer of the county court records from it to "New Town," present site of downtown San Diego, on the night of March 31, 1871.

Despite threats to forcibly prevent even legal transfer of the court house to "New Town," Col. Chalmers Scott, then county clerk and recorder, and his henchmen removed the county records under cover of darkness and transported them to a "New Town" building at 6th and G Streets.

The Whaley House would be gone today but for a group of San Diegans who prevented its demolition in 1956 by forming the Historical Shrine Foundation of San Diego County and buying the land and the building.

Later, the group convinced the County of San Diego that the house should be preserved as an historical museum, and restored to its early-day splendor. This was done under the supervision and guidance of an advisory committee including members of the Foundation, which today maintains the Whaley House as an historical museum.

Most of the furnishings, authenticated as in use in Whaley's time, are from other early-day San Diego County homes and were donated by interested citizens.

The last Whaley to live in the house was Corinne Lillian Whaley, youngest of Whaley's six children. She died at the age of 89 in 1953. Whaley himself died December 14, 1890, at the age of 67. He is buried in San Diego in Mount Hope Cemetery, as is his wife, Anna, who lived until February 24, 1913.

When it became apparent that a thorough investigation of the haunting would be made, and that all of San Diego would be able to learn of it through television and newspapers, excitement mounted to a high pitch.

Mrs. Reading kept in close touch with Regis and me because ghosts have a way of "sensing" an impending attempt to oust them—and this was not long in coming. On May 24th the "activities" inside the house had already increased to a marked degree; they were of the same general nature as previously noticed sounds.

Was the ghost getting restless?

I had asked Mrs. Reading to prepare an exact account of all occurrences within the house, from the very first moment on, and to assemble as many of the witnesses as possible for further interrogation.

Most of these people had worked part time as guides in the house during the five years since its restoration. The phenomena thus far had occurred, or at any rate been observed, mainly between 10 A.M. and 5:30 P.M., when the house is open to visitors. There is no one there at night, but an effective burglar alarm system is in operation to prevent flesh-and-blood intruders from breaking in unnoticed. Ineffective with the ghostly kind, as we were soon to learn!

I shall now quote the director's own report. It vouches for the accuracy and calibre of witnesses.

Phenomena Observed at Whaley House
By Visitors

Oct. 9, 1960—Dr. & Mrs. Kirbey of New Westminster, B.C., Canada. 1:30–2:30 P.M. (He was then Director of the Medical Association of New Westminster.)

While Dr. Kirbey and his wife were in the house, he became interested in an exhibit in one of the display cases and his wife asked if she might go through the rest of the house by herself, because she was familiar with the Victorian era, and felt very much at home in these surroundings. Accordingly, I remained downstairs with the Doctor, discussing early physicians and medical practices.

When Mrs. Kirbey returned to the display room, she asked me in hesitating fashion if I had ever noticed anything unusual about the upstairs. I asked her what she had noticed. She reported that when she started upstairs, she felt a breeze over her head, and though she saw nothing, realized a pressure against her seemed to make it hard to go up. When she looked into the rooms, had the feeling that someone was standing behind her, in fact so close to her that she turned around several times to look. Said she expected someone would tap her on the shoulder. When she joined us downstairs, we all walked toward the courtroom. As we entered, again Mrs. Kirbey turned to me and asked if I knew that someone inhabited the courtroom. She pointed to the bailiff's table, saying as she did, "Right over there." I asked her if the person was clear enough for her to describe, and she said:

"I see a small figure of a woman who has a swarthy complexion. She is wearing a long full skirt, reaching to the floor. The skirt appears to be a calico or gingham, small print. She has a kind of cap on her head, dark hair and eyes and she is wearing gold hoops in her pierced ears. She seems to stay in this room, lives here, I gather, and I get the impression we are sort of invading her privacy."

Mrs. Kirbey finished her description by asking me if any of the Whaley family were swarthy, to which I replied, "No."

This was, to my knowledge, the only description given of an apparition by a visitor, and Mrs. Kirbey the only person who brought up the fact in connection with the courtroom. Many of the visitors have commented upon the atmosphere in this room, however, and some people attempting to work in the room comment upon the difficulty they have in trying to concentrate here.

By Persons Employed at Whaley House

April, 1960
10:00 A.M. By myself, June A. Reading, 3447 Kite St.
Sound of Footsteps—in the Upstairs

This sound of someone walking across the floor, I first heard in the morning, a week before the museum opened to the public. County workmen were still painting some shelving in the hall, and during this week often arrived before I did, so it was not unusual to find them already at work when I arrived.

This morning, however, I was planning to furnish the downstairs rooms, and so hurried in and down the hall to open the back door awaiting the arrival of the trucks with the furnishings. Two men followed me down the hall; they were going to help with the furniture arrangement. As I reached up to unbolt the back door, I heard the sound of what seemed to be someone walking across the bedroom floor. I paid no attention, thinking it was one of the workmen. But the men, who heard the sounds at the time I did, insisted I go upstairs and find out who was in the house. So, calling out, I started to mount the stairs. Halfway up, I could see no lights, and that the outside shutters to the windows were still closed. I made some comment to the men who had followed me, and turned around to descend the stairs. One of the men joked with me about the spirits coming in to look things over, and we promptly forgot the matter.

However, the sound of walking continued. And for the next six months I found myself going upstairs to see if someone was actually upstairs. This would happen during the day, sometimes when visitors were in other parts of the house, other times when I was busy at my desk trying to catch up on correspondence or bookwork. At times it would sound as though someone were descending the stairs, but would fade away before reaching the first floor. In September, 1962, the house was the subject of a news article in the *San Diego Evening Tribune*, and this same story was reprinted in the September 1962 issue of *Fate* magazine.

Oct. & Nov. 1962. We began to have windows in the upper part of the house open unaccountably. We installed horizontal bolts on three windows in the front bedroom, thinking this would end the matter. However, the really disturbing part of this came when it set off our burglar alarm in the night, and we were called by the Police and San Diego Burglar Alarm Co. to come down and see if the house had been broken into. Usually, we would find nothing disturbed. (One exception to this was when the house was broken into by vandals, about 1963, and items from the kitchen display stolen.)

In the fall of 1962, early October, while engaged in giving a talk to some school children, a class of 25 pupils, I heard a sound of someone walking, which seemed to come from the roof. One of the children interrupted me, asking what that noise was, and excusing myself from them, I went outside the building, down on the street to see if workmen from the County were repairing the roof. Satisfied that there was no one on the roof of the building, I went in and resumed the tour.

Residents of Old Town are familiar with this sound, and

tell me that it has been evident for years. Miss Whaley, who lived in the house for 85 years, was aware of it. She passed away in 1953.

Mrs. Grace Bourquin, 2938 Beech St.

Sat. Dec. 14, 1963, noon—Was seated in the hall downstairs having lunch, when she heard walking sound in upstairs.

Sat. Jan. 10, 1964, 1:30 P.M. Walked down the hall and looked up the staircase. On the upper landing she saw an apparition—the figure of a man, clad in frock coat and pantaloons, the face turned away from her, so she could not make it out. Suddenly it faded away.

Lawrence Riveroll, resides on Jefferson St., Old Town.

Jan. 5, 1963, 12:30 noon

Was alone in the house. No visitors present at the time. While seated at a desk in the front hall, heard sounds of music and singing, described as a woman's voice. Song "Home Again." Lasted about 30 seconds.

Jan. 7, 1963, 1:30 P.M.

Visitors in upstairs. Downstairs, he heard organ music, which seemed to come from the courtroom, where there is an organ. Walked into the room to see if someone was attempting to play it. Cover on organ was closed. He saw no one in the room.

Jan. 19, 1963, 5:15 P.M.

Museum was closed for the day. Engaged in closing shutters downstairs. Heard footsteps in upper part of house in the same area as described. Went up to check, saw nothing.

Sept. 10–12, 1964—at dusk, about 5:15 P.M.

Engaged in closing house, together with another worker. Finally went into the music room, began playing the piano.

Suddenly felt a distinct pressure on his hands, as though someone had their hands on his. He turned to look toward the front hall, in the direction of the desk, hoping to get the attention of the person seated there, when he saw the apparition of a slight woman dressed in a hoop skirt. In the dim light was unable to see clearly the face. Suddenly the figure vanished.

J. Milton Keller, 4114 Middlesex Dr.

Sept. 22, 1964, 2:00 P.M.
Engaged in tour with visitors at the parlor, when suddenly he, together with people assembled at balustrade, noticed crystal drops hanging from lamp on parlor table begin to swing back and forth. This occurred only on one side of the lamp. The other drops did not move. This continued about two minutes.

Dec. 15, 1964, 5:15 P.M.
Engaged in closing house along with others. Returned from securing restrooms, walked down hall, turned to me with the key, while I stepped into the hall closet to reach for the master switch which turns off all lights. I pulled the switch, started to turn around to step out, when he said, "Stop, don't move, you'll step on the dog!" He put his hands out, in a gesture for me to stay still. Meantime, I turned just in time to see what resembled a flash of light between us, and what appeared to be the back of a dog, scurry down the hall and turn into the dining room. I decided to resume a normal attitude, so I kidded him a little about trying to scare me. Other people were present in the front hall at the time, waiting for us at the door, so he turned to them and said in a rather hurt voice that I did not believe him. I realized then that he had witnessed an apparition, so I asked him to see if he could describe it. *He said he saw a spotted dog, like a fox terrier, that ran with his ears flapping, down the hall and into the dining room.*

Dec. 27, 1964, 5:00 P.M.

Late afternoon, prior to closing, *saw the apparition of a woman dressed in a green plaid gingham dress.* She had long dark hair, coiled up in a bun at neck, was seated on a settee in bedroom.

Feb. 1965, 2:00 P.M.

Engaged in giving a tour with visitors, when two elderly ladies called and asked him to come upstairs, and step over to the door of the nursery. These ladies, visitors, called his attention to a sound that was like the cry of a baby, about 16 months old. All three reported the sound.

March 24, 1965, 1:00 P.M.

He, together with Mrs. Bourquin and his parents, Mr. & Mrs. Keller, engaged in touring the visitors, when for some reason his attention was directed to the foot of the staircase. He walked back to it, and heard the sound of someone in the upper part of the house whistling. No one was in the upstairs at the time.

May 29, 1965, 2:30 P.M.

Escorting visitors through house, upstairs. Called to me, asking me to come up. Upon going up, he, I and visitors all witnessed a black rocking chair, moving back and forth as if occupied by a person. It had started moving unaccountably, went on about three minutes. Caused quite a stir among visitors.

Mrs. Suzanne Pere, 106 Albatross, El Cajon.

April 8, 1963, 4:30 P.M.

Was engaged in typing in courtroom, working on manuscript. Suddenly she called to me, calling my attention to a noise in the upstairs. We both stopped work, walked up the stairs together, to see if anyone could possibly be there. As it was near closing time, we decided to secure the windows. Mrs. Pere kept noticing a chilly breeze at the back of her head, had the distinct feeling that someone, though invisible, was present and kept following her from one window to another.

Oct. 7, 1963, 10:30 A.M.

Reported unaccountable sounds issuing from kitchen, as though someone were at work there. Same day, she reported smelling the odor of something baking.

Nov. 28, 1963, 2:30 P.M.

Reported seeing an apparition in the study. A group of men there, dressed in frock coats, some with plain vests, others figured material. One of this group had a large gold watch chain across vest. Seemed to be a kind of meeting; all figures were animated, some pacing the floor, others conversing; all serious and agitated, but oblivious to everything else. One figure in this group seemed to be an official, and stood off by himself. This person was of medium stocky build, light brown hair, and mustache which was quite full and long. He had very piercing light blue eyes, penetrating gaze. Mrs. Pere sensed that he was some kind of official, a person of importance. He seemed about to speak. Mrs. Pere seemed quite exhausted by her experience witnessing this scene, yet was quite curious about the man with the penetrating gaze. I remember her asking me if I knew of anyone answering this description, because it remained with her for some time.

Oct. 14, 21; Nov. 18, 1964

During the morning and afternoon on these days, she called my attention to the smell of cigar smoke, and the fragrance of perfume or cologne. This occurred in the parlor, hall, upstairs bedroom. In another bedroom she called my attention to something resembling dusting powder.

Nov. 27, 1964, 10:15 A.M.

Heard a distinct noise from kitchen area, as though something had dropped to the floor. I was present when this occurred. She called to me and asked what I was doing there, thinking I had been rearranging exhibits. At this time I was at work in the courtroom, laying out work. Both of us reached the kitchen, to find one of the utensils on the shelf rack had disengaged itself, fallen to the floor, and had struck a copper boiler directly below. We were at a loss to explain this. No one else was in the house at the time.

Mrs. T. R. Allen, 3447 Kite Street.

Was present *Jan. 7, 1963,* 1:30 P.M. Heard organ music issue from courtroom, when Lawrence Riveroll heard the same (see his statement).

Was present *Sept. 10–12, 1964,* at dusk, with Lawrence Riveroll, when he witnessed apparition. Mrs. Allen went upstairs to close shutters, and as she ascended them, described a chill breeze that seemed to come over her head. Upstairs, she walked into the bedroom and toward the windows. Suddenly she heard a sound behind her, as though something had dropped to the floor. She turned to look, saw nothing, but again experienced the feeling of having someone, invisible, hovering near her. She had a feeling of fear. Completed her task as quickly as possible, and left the upstairs hastily. Upon my return, both persons seemed anxious to leave the house.

May, 1965 (the last Friday), 1:30 P.M.

Was seated in downstairs front hall, when she heard the sound of footsteps.

Regis had been to the house before. With him on that occasion were Mrs. Philbin, who is highly sensitive to psychic emanations, and a teacher-friend of theirs, who is considered an amateur medium.

They observed, during their vigil, what appeared to be a white figure of a person, but when Regis challenged it with his flashlight, it disappeared immediately. Mrs. Philbin felt extremely uncomfortable on that occasion and had no desire to return to the house.

By now I knew that the house had four ghosts, a man, a woman, a baby—and a spotted dog. The scene observed in one of the rooms sounded more like a psychic impression of a past event to me than a bona fide ghost.

I later discovered that still another part-time guide at the house, William H. Richardson, of 470 Silvery Lane, El Cajon, had not only experienced something out of the ordinary at the house, but had taken part in a kind of séance with interesting results. Here is his statement, given to me in September of 1965, several months *after* our own trance session had taken place.

In the summer of 1963 I worked in Whaley House as a guide.

One morning before the house was open to the public, several of us employees were seated in the music room downstairs, and the sound of someone in heavy boots walking across the upstairs was heard by us all. When we went to investigate the noise, we found all the windows locked and shuttered, and the only door to the outside from upstairs was locked. This experience first sparked my interest in ghosts.

I asked June Reading, the director, to allow several of my friends from Starlight Opera, a local summer musical theater, to spend the night in the house.

At midnight, on Friday, August 13, we met at the house. Carolyn Whyte, a member of the parapsychology group in San Diego and a member of the Starlight Chorus, gave an introductory talk on what to expect, and we all went into the parlor to wait for something to happen.

The first experience was that of a cool breeze blowing through the room, which was felt by several of us despite the fact that all doors and windows were locked and shuttered.

The next thing that happened was that a light appeared over a boy's head. This traveled from his head across the wall, where it disappeared. Upon later investigation it was found to have disappeared at the portrait of Thomas Whaley, the original owner of the house. Footsteps were also heard several times in the room upstairs.

At this point we broke into groups and dispersed to different parts of the house. One group went into the study which is adjacent to the parlor, and there witnessed a shadow on the wall surrounded by a pale light which moved up and down the wall and changed shape as it did so. There was no source of light into the room and one could pass in front of the shadow without disturbing it.

Another group was upstairs when their attention was directed simultaneously to the chandelier which began to swing around as if someone were holding the bottom and twisting the sides. One boy was tapped on the leg several times by some unseen force while seated there.

Meanwhile, downstairs in the parlor, an old-fashioned lamp with prisms hanging on the edges began to act strangely. As we watched, several prisms began to swing by themselves. These would stop and others would start, but they never swung simultaneously. There was no breeze in the room.

At this time we all met in the courtroom. Carolyn then suggested that we try to lift the large table in the room.

We sat around the table and placed our fingertips on it. A short while later it began to creak and then slid across the floor approximately eight inches, and finally lifted completely off the floor on the corner where I was seated.

Later on we brought a small table from the music room into the courtroom and tried to get it to tip, which it did. With just our fingertips on it, it tilted until it was approximately one inch from the floor, then fell. We righted the table and put our fingertips back on it, and almost immediately it began to rock. Since we knew the code for yes, no, and doubtful, we began to converse with the table. Incidentally, while this was going on, a chain across the doorway in the courtroom was almost continually swinging back and forth and then up and down.

Through the system of knocking, we discovered that the ghost was that of a little girl, seven years old. She did not tell us her name, but she did tell us that she had red hair, freckles, and hazel eyes. She also related that there were four other ghosts in the house besides herself, including that of a baby boy. We conversed with her spirit for nearly an hour.

At one time the table stopped rocking and started moving across the floor of the courtroom, into the dining room, through the pantry, and into the kitchen. This led us to believe that the kitchen was her usual abode. The table then stopped and several antique kitchen utensils on the wall began to swing violently. Incidentally, the kitchen utensils swung for the rest of the evening at different intervals.

The table then retraced its path back to the courtroom and answered more questions.

At 5:00 A.M. we decided to call it a night—a most interesting night. When we arrived our group of 15 had had in it a couple of real believers, several who half believed, and quite a few who didn't believe at all. After the phenomena we had experienced, there was not one among us who was even a little doubtful in the belief of some form of existence after life.

It was Friday evening, and time to meet the ghosts. Sybil knew nothing whatever about the house, and when Regis picked us up the conversation remained polite and non-ghostly.

When we arrived at the house, word of mouth had preceded us despite the fact that our plans had not been announced publicly; certainly it had not been advertised that we would attempt a séance that evening. Nevertheless, a sizable crowd had assembled at the house and only Regis's polite insistence that their presence might harm whatever results we could obtain made them move on.

It was quite dark now, and I followed Sybil into the house, allowing her to get her clairvoyant bearings first, prior to the trance session we were to do with the cameras rolling. My wife Catherine trailed right behind me carrying the tape equipment. Mrs. Reading received us cordially. The witnesses had assembled but were temporarily out of reach, so that Sybil could not gather any sensory impressions from them. They patiently waited through our clairvoyant tour. All in all, about a dozen people awaited us. The house was lit throughout and the excitement in the atmosphere was bound to stir up any ghost present!

And so it was that on June 25, 1965, the Ghost Hunter came to close quarters with the specters at Whaley House, San Diego. While Sybil meandered about the house by herself, I quickly went over to the Court House part of the house and went over their experiences with the witnesses. Although I already had their statements, I wanted to make sure no detail had escaped me.

From Mrs. Reading I learned, for instance, that the winds are standard with traditional hauntings, but here we had a precise witness to testify.

"It was cold and I was chilly all over. And another thing, when I lock the shutters upstairs at night, I feel like someone is breathing down the back of my neck, like they're going to touch me—at the shoulder—that happened often. Why only a month ago."

A Mrs. Frederick Bear now stepped forward. I could not find her name in Mrs. Reading's brief report. Evidently she was an additional witness to the uncanny goings-on at this house.

"One evening I came here—it was after five o'clock; another lady was here also—and June Reading was coming down the stairs, and we were talking. I distinctly heard something move upstairs, as if someone were moving a table. There was no one there—we checked. That only happened a month ago."

Grace Bourquin, another volunteer worker at the house, had been touched upon in Mrs. Reading's report. She emphasized that the sounds were those of a heavy man wearing boots—no mistake about it. When I questioned her about the apparition of a man she had seen, about six weeks ago, wearing a frock coat, she insisted that he had looked like a real person to her, standing at the top of the stairs one moment, and completely gone the next.

"He did not move. I saw him clearly, then turned my head for a second to call out to Mrs. Reading, and when I looked again, he had disappeared."

I had been fascinated by Mrs. Suzanne Pere's account of her experiences, which seemed to indicate a large degree of mediumship in her makeup. I questioned her about anything she had not yet told us.

"On one occasion June Reading and I were in the back study and working with the table. We had our hands on the table to see if we could get any reaction."

"You mean you were trying to do some table-tipping."

"Yes. At this point I had only had some feelings in the house, and smelled some cologne. This was about a year ago, and we were working with some papers concerning the Indian uprising in San Diego, and all of a sudden the table started to rock violently! All of the pulses in my body became throbbing, and in my mind's eye the room was filled with men, all of them extremely excited, and though I could not hear any sound, I knew they were talking, and one gentleman was striding up and down the center of the room, puffing on his cigar, and from my description of him June Reading later identified him as Sheriff McCoy, who was here in the 1850s. When it was finished I could not talk for a few minutes, I was completely disturbed for a moment."

McCoy, I found, was the leader of one of the factions during the "battle" between Old Town and New Town San Diego for the county seat.

Evidently, Mrs. Bourquin had psychically relived that emotion-laden event which did indeed transpire in the very room she saw it!

"Was the Court House ever used to execute anyone?" I interjected.

Mrs. Reading was not sure; the records were all there but the Historical Society had not gone over them as yet for lack of staff. The Court functioned in this house for two years, however, and sentences certainly were meted out in it. The prison itself was a bit farther up the street.

A lady in a red coat caught my attention. She identified herself as Bernice Kennedy.

"I'm a guide here Sundays," the lady began, "and one Sunday

recently, I was alone in the house and sitting in the dining room reading, and I heard the front door open and close. There was no one there. I went back to continue my reading. Then I heard it the second time. Again I checked, and there was absolutely no one there. I heard it a third time and this time I took my book and sat outside at the desk. From then onward, people started to come in and I had no further unusual experience. But one other Sunday, there was a young woman upstairs who came down suddenly very pale, and she said the little rocking chair upstairs was rocking. I followed the visitor up and I could not see the chair move, but there was a clicking sound, very rhythmic, and I haven't heard it before or since."

The chair, it came out, once belonged to a family related to the Whaleys.

"I'm Charles Keller, father of Milton Keller," a booming voice said behind me, and an imposing gentleman in his middle years stepped forward.

"I once conducted a tour through the Whaley House. I noticed a lady who had never been here act as if she were being pushed out of one of the bedrooms!"

"Did you see it?" I said, somewhat taken aback.

"Yes," Mr. Keller nodded, "I saw her move, as if someone were pushing her out of the room."

"Did you interrogate her about it?"

"Yes, I did. It was only in the first bedroom, where we started the tour, that it happened. Not in any of the other rooms. We went back to that room and again I saw her being pushed out of it!"

Mrs. Keller then spoke to me about the ice-cold draft she felt, and just before that, three knocks at the back door! Her son, whose testimony Mrs. Reading had already obtained for me, then went to the back door and found no one there who could have knocked. This had happened only six months before our visit.

I then turned to James Reading, the head of the Association responsible for the upkeep of the museum and house, and asked for his own encounters with the ghosts. Mr. Reading, in a cautious tone, explained that he did not really cotton to ghosts, but—

"The house was opened to the public in April 1960. In the fall of that year, October or November, the police called me at two o'clock in the morning, and asked me to please go down and shut off the burglar alarm, because they were being flooded with complaints, it was waking up everybody in the neighborhood. I came down and found two officers waiting for me. I shut off the alarm. They had meantime checked the house and every door and shutter was tight."

"How could the alarm have gone off by itself then?"

"I don't know. I unlocked the door, and we searched the entire house. When we finally got upstairs, we found one of the upstairs front bedroom windows open. We closed and bolted the window, and came down and tested the alarm. It was in order again. No one could have gotten in or out. The shutters outside that window were closed and hooked on the inside. The opening of the window had set off the alarm, but it would have been impossible for anyone to open that window and get either into or out of the house. Impossible. This happened *four times*. The second time, about four months later, again at two in the morning, again that same window was standing open. The other two times it was always that same window."

"What did you finally do about it?"

"After the fourth incident we added a second bolt at right angles to the first one, and that seemed to help. There were no further calls."

Was the ghost getting tired of pushing *two* bolts out of the way?

I had been so fascinated with all this additional testimony that I had let my attention wander away from my favorite medium, Sybil Leek. But now I started to look for her and found to my amazement that she had seated herself in one of the old chairs in what used to be the kitchen, downstairs in back of the living room. When I entered the room she seemed deep in thought, although not in trance by any means, and yet it took me a while to make her realize where we were.

Had anything unusual transpired while I was in the Court Room interviewing?

"I was standing in the entrance hall, looking at the postcards," Sybil recollected, "when I felt I just had to go to the kitchen, but I didn't go there at first, but went halfway up the stairs, and a child came down the stairs and into the kitchen and I followed her."

"A child?" I asked. I was quite sure there were no children among our party.

"I thought it was Regis's little girl and the next thing I recall I was in the rocking chair and you were saying something to me."

Needless to say, Regis Philbin's daughter had *not* been on the stairs. I asked for a detailed description of the child.

"It was a long-haired girl," Sybil said. "She was very quick, you know, in a longish dress. She went to the table in this room and I went to the chair. That's all I remember."

I decided to continue to question Sybil about any psychic impressions she might now gather in the house.

"There is a great deal of confusion in this house," she began. "Some of it is associated with another room upstairs, which has been structurally altered. There are two centers of activity."

Sybil, of course, could not have known that the house consisted of two separate units.

"Any ghosts in the house?"

"Several," Sybil assured me. "At least four!"

Had not William Richardson's group made contact with a little girl ghost who had claimed that she knew of four other ghosts in the house? The report of that séance did not reach me until September, several months after our visit, so Sybil could not possibly have "read our minds" about it, since our minds had no such knowledge at that time.

"This room where you found me sitting," Sybil continued, "I found myself drawn to it; the impressions are very strong here. Especially that child—she died young."

We went about the house now, seeking further contacts.

"I have a date now," Sybil suddenly said, "1872."

The Readings exchanged significant glances. It was just after the greatest bitterness of the struggle between Old Town and New Town, when the removal of the Court records from Whaley House by force occurred.

"There are two sides to the house," Sybil continued. "One side I like, but not the other."

Rather than have Sybil use up her energies in clairvoyance, I felt it best to try for a trance in the Court Room itself. This was quickly arranged, with candles taking the place of electric lights except for what light was necessary for the motion picture cameras in the rear of the large room.

Regis and I sat at Sybil's sides as she slumped forward in a chair that may well have held a merciless judge in bygone years.

But the first communicator was neither the little girl nor the man in the frock coat. A feeble, plaintive voice was suddenly heard from Sybil's lips, quite unlike her own, a voice evidently parched with thirst.

"Bad . . . fever . . . everybody had the fever . . ."

"What year is this?"

"Forty-six."

I suggested that the fever had passed, and generally calmed the personality who did not respond to my request for identification.

"Send me . . . some water. . . ." Sybil was still in trance, but herself now. Immediately she complained about there being a lot of confusion.

"This isn't the room where we're needed . . . the child . . . she is the one. . . ."

"What is her name?"

"Anna . . . Bell . . . she died very suddenly with something, when she was thirteen . . . chest. . . ."

"Are her parents here too?"

"They come . . . the lady comes."

"What is this house used for?"

"Trade . . . selling things, buying and selling."

"Is there anyone other than the child in this house?"

"Child is the main one, because she doesn't understand anything at all. But there is something more vicious. Child would not hurt anyone. There's someone else. A man. He knows something about this house . . . about thirty-two, unusual name, C . . . Calstrop . . . five feet ten, wearing a green coat, darkish, mustache and side whiskers, he goes up to the bedroom on the left. He has business here. His business is with things that come from the sea. But it is the papers that worry him."

"What papers?" I demanded.

"The papers . . . 1872. About the house. Dividing the house was wrong. Two owners, he says."

"What is the house being used for, now, in 1872?"

"To live in. Two places. . . I get confused for I go one place and then I have to go to another."

"Did this man you see die here?"

"He died here. Unhappy because of the place . . . about the other place. Two buildings. Some people quarrelled about the spot. He is laughing. He wants all this house for himself."

"Does he know he is dead?" I asked the question that often brings forth much resistance to my quest for facts from those who cannot conceive of their status as "ghosts."

Sybil listened for a moment.

"He does as he wants in this house because he is going to live here," she finally said. "*It's his house.*"

"Why is he laughing?"

A laughing ghost, indeed!

"He laughs because of people coming here thinking it's *their* house! When he knows the truth."

"What is his name?" I asked again.

"Cal . . . Caltrop . . . very difficult as he does not speak very clearly . . . he writes and writes . . . he makes a noise . . . he says he will make even more noise unless you go away."

"Let him," I said, cheerfully hoping I could tape-record the ghost's outburst.

"Tell him he has passed over and the matter is no longer important," I told Sybil.

"He is upstairs."

I asked that he walk upstairs so we could all hear him. There was nobody upstairs at this moment—everybody was watching the proceedings in the Court Room downstairs.

We kept our breath, waiting for the manifestations, but our ghost wouldn't play the game. I continued with my questions.

"What does he want?"

"He is just walking around, he can do as he likes," Sybil said. "He does not like new things . . . he does not like any noise . . . except when he makes it. . . ."

"Who plays the organ in this house?"

"He says his mother plays."

"What is her name?"

"Ann Lassay . . . that's wrong, it's Lann—he speaks so badly . . . Lannay . . . his throat is bad or something. . . ."

I later was able to check on this unusual name. Anna Lannay was Thomas Whaley's wife!

At the moment, however, I was not aware of this fact and pressed on with my interrogation. How did the ghost die? How long ago?

"'89 . . . he does not want to speak; he only wants to roam around. . . ."

Actually, Whaley died in 1890. Had the long interval confused his sense of time? So many ghosts cannot recall exact dates but will remember circumstances and emotional experiences well.

"He worries about the house . . . he wants the whole house . . . for himself . . . he says he will leave them . . . papers . . . hide the papers . . . he wants the other papers about the house . . . they're four miles from here . . . several people have these papers and you'll have to get them back or he'll never settle . . . never . . . and if he doesn't get the whole house back, he will be much worse . . .

and then, the police will come . . . he will make the lights come and the noise . . . and the bell . . . make the police come and see him, the master . . . of the house, he hears bells upstairs . . . he doesn't know what it is . . . he goes upstairs and opens the windows, wooden windows . . . and looks out . . . and then he pulls the . . . no, it's not a bell . . . he'll do it again . . . when he wants someone to know that he really is the master of the house . . . people today come and say he is not, but he is!"

I was surprised. Sybil had no knowledge of the disturbances, the alarm bell, the footsteps, the open window . . . and yet it was all perfectly true. Surely, her communicator was our man!

"When did he do this the last time?" I inquired.

"This year . . . not long. . . ."

"Has he done anything else in this house?"

"He said he moved the lights. In the parlor."

Later I thought of the Richardson séance and the lights they had observed, but of course I had no idea of this when we were at the house ourselves.

"What about the front door?"

"If people come, he goes into the garden . . . walks around . . . because he meets mother there."

"What is in the kitchen?"

"Child goes to the kitchen. I have to leave him, and he doesn't want to be left . . . it was an injustice, anyway, don't like it . . . the child is twelve . . . chest trouble . . . something from the kitchen . . . bad affair. . . ."

"Anyone's fault?"

"Yes. Not chest . . . from the cupboard, took something . . . it was an acid like salt, and she ate it . . . she did not know . . . there is something strange about this child, someone had control of her, you see, she was in the way . . . family . . . one girl . . . those boys were not too good . . . the other boys who came down . . . she is like two people . . . someone controlled her . . . made her do strange things and then . . . could she do that. . . ."

"Was she the daughter of the man?"

"Strange man, he doesn't care so much about the girl as he does about the house. He is disturbed."

"Is there a woman in this house?"

"Of course. There is a woman in the garden."

"Who is she?"

"Mother. Grandmother of the girl."

"Is he aware of the fact he has no physical body?"

"No."

"Doesn't he see all the people who come here?"

"They have to be fought off, sent away."

"Tell him it is now seventy years later."

"He says seventy years when the house was built."

"Another seventy years have gone by," I insisted. "Only part of you is in the house."

"No, part of the house . . . you're making the mistake," he replied.

I tried hard to convince him of the real circumstances. Finally, I assured him that the entire house was, in effect, his.

Would this help?

"He is vicious," Sybil explains. "He will have his revenge on the house."

I explained that his enemies were all dead.

"He says it was an injustice, and the Court was wrong and you have to tell everyone this is his house and land and home."

I promised to do so and intoned the usual formula for the release of earthbound people who have passed over and don't realize it. Then I recalled Sybil to her own self, and within a few moments she was indeed in full control.

I then turned to the director of the museum, Mrs. Reading, and asked for her comments on the truth of the material just heard.

"There was a litigation," she said. "The injustice could perhaps refer to the County's occupancy of this portion of the house from 1869 to 1871. Whaley's contract, which we have, shows that this portion of the house was leased to the County, and he was to supply the furniture and set it up as a Court Room. He also put in the two windows to provide light. It was a valid agreement. They adhered to the contract as long as the Court continued to function here, but when Alonzo Horton came and developed New Town, a hot contest began between the two communities for the possession of the county seat. When the records were forcefully removed from here, Whaley felt it was quite an injustice, and we have letters he addressed to the Board of Supervisors, referring to the fact that his lease had been broken. The Clerk notified him that they were no longer responsible for the use of this house—after all the work he had put in to remodel it for their use. He would bring the matter up periodically with the Board of Supervisors, but it was tabled by them each time it came up."

"In other words, this is the injustice referred to by the ghost?"

"In 1872 he was bitterly engaged in asking redress from the County over this matter, which troubled him some since he did not believe a government official would act in this manner. It was never settled, however, and Whaley was left holding the bag."

"Was there a child in the room upstairs?"

"In the nursery? There were several children there. One child died here. But this was a boy."

Again, later, I saw that the Richardson séance spoke of a boy ghost in the house.

At the very beginning of trance, before I began taping the utterances from Sybil's lips, I took some handwritten notes. The personality, I now saw, who had died of a bad fever had given the faintly pronounced name of Fedor and spoke of a mill where he worked. Was there any sense to this?

"Yes," Mrs. Reading confirmed, "this room we are in now served as a granary at one time. About 1855 to 1867."

"Were there ever any Russians in this area?"

"There was a considerable otter trade here prior to the American occupation of the area. We have found evidence that the Russians established wells in this area. They came into these waters then to trade otters."

"Amazing," I conceded. How could Sybil, even if she wanted to, have known of such an obscure fact?

"This would have been in the 1800s," Mrs. Reading continued. "Before then there were Spaniards here, of course."

"Anything else you wish to comment upon in the trance session you have just witnessed?" I asked.

Mrs. Reading expressed what we all felt.

"The references to the windows opening upstairs, and the ringing of these bells. . . ."

How could Sybil have known all that? Nobody told her and she had not had a chance to acquaint herself with the details of the disturbances.

What remained were the puzzling statements about "the other house." They, too, were soon to be explained. We were walking through the garden now and inspected the rear portion of the Whaley house. In back of it, we discovered to our surprise still another wooden house standing in the garden. I questioned Mrs. Reading about this second house.

"The Pendington House, in order to save it, had to be moved out of the path of the freeway . . . it never belonged to the Whaleys although Thomas Whaley once tried to rent it. But it was always rented to someone else."

No wonder the ghost was angry about "the other house." It had been moved and put on *his* land . . . without his consent!

The name *Cal . . . trop* still did not fall into place. It was too far removed from Whaley and yet everything else that had come through Sybil clearly fitted Thomas Whaley. Then the light began to dawn, thanks to Mrs. Reading's detailed knowledge of the house.

"It was interesting to hear Mrs. Leek say there was a store here once . . ." she explained. "This is correct, there was a store here at one time, but it was not Mr. Whaley's."

"Whose was it?"

"It belonged to a man named Wallack . . . Hal Wallack . . . that was in the seventies."

Close enough to Sybil's tentative pronunciation of a name she caught connected with the house.

"He rented it to Wallack for six months, then Wallack sold out," Mrs. Reading explained.

I also discovered, in discussing the case with Mrs. Reading, that the disturbances really began after the second house had been placed on the grounds. Was that the straw that broke the ghost's patience?

Later we followed Sybil to a wall adjoining the garden, a wall, I should add, where there was no visible door. But Sybil insisted there had been a French window there, and indeed there was at one time. In a straight line from this spot, we wound up at a huge tree. It was here, Sybil explained, that Whaley and his mother often met—or are meeting, as the case may be.

I was not sure that Mr. Whaley had taken my advice to heart and moved out of what was, after all, his house. Why should he? The County had not seen fit to undo an old wrong.

We left the next morning, hoping that at the very least we had let the restless one know someone cared.

A week later Regis Philbin checked with the folks at Whaley House. Everything was lively—chandelier swinging, rocker rocking; and June Reading herself brought me up to date on July 27, 1965, with a brief report on activities—other than flesh-and-blood—at the house.

Evidently the child ghost was still around, for utensils in the kitchen had moved that week, especially a cleaver which swings back and forth on its own. Surely that must be the playful little girl, for what would do important a man as Thomas Whaley have to do in the kitchen? Surely he was much too preoccupied with the larger aspects of his realm, the ancient wrong done him, and the many intrusions from the world of reality. For the Whaley House is a busy place, ghosts or not.

On replaying my tapes, I noticed a curious confusion between the initial appearance of a ghost who called himself Fedor in my notes, and a man who said he had a bad fever. It was just that the man with the fever did not have a foreign accent, but I distinctly recalled "fedor" as sounding odd.

Were they perhaps two separate entities?

My suspicions were confirmed when a letter written May 23, 1966—almost a year later—reached me. A Mrs. Carol DeJuhasz wanted me to know about a ghost at Whaley House . . . no, not Thomas Whaley or a twelve-year-old girl with long hair. Mrs. DeJuhasz was concerned with an historical play written by a friend of hers, dealing with the unjust execution of a man who tried to steal a harbor boat in the 1800s and was caught. Make no mistake about it, nobody had observed this ghost at Whaley House. Mrs. DeJuhasz merely thought he ought to be there, having been hanged in the backyard of the house.

Many people tell me of tragic spots where men have died unhappily but rarely do I discover ghosts on such spots. I was therefore not too interested in Mrs. DeJuhasz's account of a possible ghost. But she thought that there ought to be present at Whaley House the ghost of this man, called Yankee Jim Robinson. When captured, he fought a saber duel and received a critical wound in the head. Although alive, he became delirious and was tried without representation, *sick of the fever.* Sentenced to death, he was subsequently hanged in the yard behind the Court House.

Was his the ghostly voice that spoke through Sybil, complaining of the fever and then quickly fading away? Again it was William Richardson who was able to provide a further clue or set of clues to this puzzle. In December of 1966 he contacted me again to report some further experiences at the Whaley House.

"This series of events began in March of this year. Our group was helping to restore an historic old house which had been moved onto the Whaley property to save it from destruction. During our lunch break one Saturday, several of us were in Whaley House. I was downstairs when Jim Stein, one of the group, rushed down the stairs to tell me that the cradle in the nursery was rocking by itself. I hurried upstairs but it wasn't rocking. I was just about to chide Jim for having an overactive imagination when it began again and rocked a little longer before it stopped. The cradle is at least ten feet from the doorway, and a metal barricade is across it to prevent tourists from entering the room. No amount of walking or jumping had any effect on the cradle. While it rocked, I remembered that it had made no sound. Going into the room, I rocked the cradle. I was surprised that it made quite a bit of noise. The old floorboards are somewhat uneven and this in combination with the wooden rockers on the cradle made a very audible sound.

"As a matter of fact, when the Whaleys were furnishing carpeting for the house, the entire upstairs portion was carpeted. This might explain the absence of the noise.

In June, Whaley House became the setting for an historical play. The play concerned the trial and hanging of a local bad man named Yankee Jim Robinson. It was presented in the Court Room and on the grounds of the mansion. The actual trial and execution had taken place in August of 1852. This was five years before Whaley House was built, but the execution took place on the grounds.

"Yankee Jim was hanged from a scaffold which stood approximately between the present music room and front parlor.

"Soon after the play went into rehearsal, things began to happen. I was involved with the production as an actor and therefore had the opportunity to spend many hours in the house between June and August. The usual footsteps kept up and they were heard by most of the members of the cast at one time or another. There was a group of us within the cast who were especially interested in the phenomenon: myself, Barry Bunker, George Carroll, and his fiancée, Toni Manista. As we were all dressed in period costumes most of the time, the ghosts should have felt right at home. Toni was playing the part of Anna, Thomas Whaley's wife. She said she often felt as if she were being followed around the house (as did we all).

"I was sitting in the kitchen with my back to the wall one night, when I felt a hand run through my hair. I quickly turned around but there was nothing to be seen. I have always felt that it was Anna Whaley who touched me. It was my first such experience and I felt honored that she had chosen me to touch. There is a chair in the kitchen which is made of rawhide and wood. The seat is made of thin strips of rawhide crisscrossed on the wooden frame. When someone sits on it, it sounds like the leather in a saddle. On the same night I was touched, the chair made sounds as if someone were sitting in it, not once but several times. There always seems to be a change in the temperature of a room when a presence enters. The kitchen is no exception. It really got cold in there!

"Later in the run of the show, the apparitions began to appear. The cast had purchased a chair which had belonged to Thomas Whaley and placed it in the front parlor. Soon after, a mist was occasionally seen in the chair or near it. In other parts of the house, especially upstairs, inexplicable shadows and mists began to appear. George Carroll swears that he saw a man standing at the top of the stairs. He walked up the stairs and through the man. The man was still there when George turned around but faded and disappeared almost immediately.

"During the summer, we often smelled cigar smoke when we opened the house in the morning or at times when no one was around. Whaley was very fond of cigars and was seldom without them.

"The footsteps became varied. The heavy steps of the man continued as usual, but the click-click of high heels was heard on occasion. Once, the sound of a small child running in the upstairs hall was heard. Another time, I was alone with the woman who took ticket reservations for *Yankee Jim*. We had locked the doors and decided to check the upstairs before we left. We had no sooner gotten up the stairs than we both heard footfalls in the hall below. We listened for a moment and then went back down the stairs and looked. No one. We searched the entire house, not really expecting to find anyone. We didn't. Not a living soul.

"Well, this just about brings you up to date. I've been back a number of times since September but there's nothing to report except the usual footfalls, creaks, etc.

"I think that the play had much to do with the summer's phenomena. Costumes, characters, and situations which were known to the Whaleys were reenacted nightly. Yankee Jim Robinson certainly has reason enough to haunt. Many people, myself included, think that he got a bad deal. He was wounded during his capture and was unconscious during most of the trial. To top it off, the judge was a drunk and the jury and townspeople wanted blood. Jim was just unlucky enough to bear their combined wrath.

"His crime? He had borrowed (?) a boat. Hardly a hanging offense. He was found guilty and condemned. He was unprepared to die and thought it was a joke up to the minute they pulled the wagon out from under him. The scaffold wasn't high enough and the fall didn't break his neck. Instead, he slowly strangled for more than fifteen minutes before he died. I think I'd haunt under the same circumstances myself.

"Two other points: another of the guides heard a voice directly in front of her as she walked down the hall. It said, 'Hello, hello.' There was no one else in the house at the time. A dog fitting the description of one of the Whaley dogs has been seen to run into the house, but it can never be found."

Usually, ghosts of different periods do not "run into" one another, unless they are tied together by a mutual problem or common tragedy. The executed man, the proud owner, the little girl, the lady of the house—they form a lively ghost population even for so roomy a house as the Whaley House.

Mrs. Reading doesn't mind. Except that it does get confusing now and again when you see someone walking about the house and aren't sure if he has bought an admission ticket.

Surely, Thomas Whaley wouldn't dream of buying one. And he is not likely to leave unless and until some action is taken publicly to rectify the ancient wrong. If the County were to reopen the matter and acknowledge the mistake made way back, I am sure the ghostly Mr. Whaley would be pleased and let matters rest. The little girl ghost has been told by Sybil Leek what has happened to her, and the lady goes where Mr. Whaley goes. Which brings us down to Jim, who would have to be tried again and found innocent of stealing the boat.

There is that splendid courtroom there at the house to do it in. Maybe some ghost-conscious county administration will see fit to do just that.

I'll be glad to serve as counsel for the accused, at no charge.

PAGES FROM MY CASEBOOK

If you're terrified by someone appearing to you out of nowhere and dissolving into thin air again making you feel the need to run away I sympathize with you. But I can't help you, and I wish you wouldn't run away. Ghosts are people, too, or they were before emotional trouble or physical trauma kept them from going on peacefully to the next plane of existence.

In the majority of cases the disturbances, ranging from noises or voices to apparitions and even physical phenomena called "poltergeists," are not meant to harm, or even frighten, you but only to get your attention. It's like a cry in the wilderness between the physical and spiritual dimensions—a cry for help to be released from whatever it is that keeps the entity attached to the place.

Once in a while, of course, a ghostly being wants you to get out of what he or she still considers its home: you are the intruder, it has rights (in its mind, anyway) and you don't. So the entity may try to induce you to leave through fear.

Take my word for it, you don't have to leave. A proper "rescue circle" with professionals should free the ghost to its next level of existence and let you stay in your own home.

But, unfortunately, few people realize this. Ghostly presences are incredibly common, though not everybody acknowledges them or wants to voice their concerns. Here is a cross section of true accounts of ghostly problems, from people like you and me. The only difference is that I would know how to resolve the matter to the satisfaction of all concerned, and in some cases I actually did.

People all over the world have moved into houses which seemed ordinary and pleasant, and spent years without ever encountering anything out of the ordinary. Then, one day, something happens to disturb their tranquility: a ghost appears, strange noises are heard, and a psychic presence makes itself known.

Why is it that phenomena occur at times long after someone moves into an affected house? Of course, there are just as many cases where the ominous presence is felt the very moment one stops across the threshold. But in cases where ghosts make their presence manifest long after the new tenants have moved in, certain conditions have not been right for such manifestations to take place at the beginning. For instance, it may involve the presence of youngsters in the household who furnish the energy for ghosts to appear. Or it may be that the shadowy entities remaining behind in the house are dimly aware of the new tenants, but wish to find out more about them before manifesting to them. Either way, once manifestations begin, the owner of the house has the choice of either ignoring them, fighting them—or coming to terms with them.

In the majority of cases, unfortunately, people simply think that the matter can be solved by ignoring the phenomena or trying hard to explain them by so-called natural causes. Ignoring problems never helps, in any area of life. When it comes to psychic phenomena, the phenomena may become worse, because even the most benighted ghost, barely aware of its predicament, will become more powerful, more restless when ignored.

• • •

Take Mrs. A.M.B., for instance. She lives in central Illinois and is by training and profession a practical nurse, engaged in psychiatric work. If anything, she can distinguish psychosis from psychic activity. She has had ESP abilities ever since she can remember. When she was twelve years old, she was playing in front of her house when she met what to her was an old man, inquiring about a certain widow living in the next block of the village. Mrs. B. knew very well that the lady had become a widow due to her husband having been killed while working as a crossing guard during a blizzard the previous winter. She remembered the man well, but the stranger did not resemble the deceased at all, so she assumed he was a relative inquiring about the dead man.

The stranger wanted to know where the widow had moved to. Mrs. B. explained that the lady had gone to visit a sister somewhere in Missouri, due to the fact, of course, that her husband had been killed in an accident. At that, the stranger nodded; he knew of the accident, he said. "Come," Mrs. B. said to the stranger, "I'll show you where another sister of the widow lives, not more than two blocks away from here. Perhaps they can tell you what town in Missouri she is visiting." The stranger obliged her, and the two were walking along the front porch, toward the steps leading down into the street, still in conversation. At that moment, her mother appeared at the front door in back of her and demanded to know what she was talking about. The girl was surprised, and explained that the gentleman was merely asking where Mrs. C. had gone, and added, "I told him she went to Missouri." But the mother replied, in a surprised tone of voice, "What are you talking about? I don't see anyone." The little girl immediately pointed at the visitor, who by that time had had enough time to get to the steps, for the front porch was rather large.

But—to her shock—she saw no one there! Immediately the girl and her mother walked into the yard, looking about everywhere without finding any trace of the strange visitor. He had simply vanished the moment the little girl had turned around to answer her mother.

• • •

Mrs. M.R. is a housewife in her late forties, living in a medium-sized New England town. Her husband works for the United States Post Office, and Mrs. R. takes care of two of their three children, the oldest being already married and living away from home. She, too, has lived with the psychic world practically from the beginning. When she was only seven years old, she and her sister, two years her senior, were in bed, playing and whispering to each other in order not to wake up their parents, whose room was next to theirs. Suddenly, there appeared a misty figure at the door connecting the children's room with the living room. It drifted through the children's room and stopped at the door to the parents' room, facing the sleeping couple. The children both saw it: the figure seemed grayish-white and had some sort of cord around its waist. At that moment their father awoke and saw it too. Yelling out to it to go away, he awoke his wife. Even though the figure still stood in the doorway of their room, she could not see it. At that moment, the ghost just disappeared.

Although Mrs. R. has had many dreams which later came true, she did not see a ghost again until she was twenty-three years old. At that time she had already given birth to her first child, and she and her husband were staying for a week at her mother's apartment. The child, having been a premature baby, was still in the hospital, and Mrs. R. lay in bed, thinking about her child. At that moment there appeared at the door to the room a very tall, dark, hooded figure. Far from being afraid, she watched the figure glide into the room, come around the foot of the bed and toward her side. The room seemed filled with a soft glow, not unlike moonlight, even though the shades were down; the furniture could be seen plainly as if there were lights in the room. By now the visitor stood right next to the bed and Mrs. R. was able to look up into his face; but in the emptiness of the hood, where a face should be, there was nothing, absolutely nothing. Then, very slowly, the figure bent over her from its great height, and it was only when the empty hood was almost touching her face, that Mrs. R. cried out in a kind of muffled way. Apparently, her outcry had broken the spell, for the phantom disappeared as quickly as it had come. Whether there was any connection between the ghostly visitor she had seen as a child and the monk-like phantom who came to her many years later, Mrs. R. does not know. But it may well be that both were one and the same, perhaps sent to protect her or guide her in some way, from out of the distant past.

· · ·

David H. is only seventeen years old and lives in Michigan. When he was eight he had his first encounter with a ghost. The house his parents lived in was more than a hundred years old, and rather large. David slept in one of two main rooms on the upper floor of the house; the room next to it was unfurnished. One night he was lying in bed when he had a sudden urge to sit up, and as he did so he looked down the hall. All of a sudden he noticed a small, shadow-like man jump down from the attic and run towards him. But instead of coming into his room, he turned down the stairs. David could see that he wore a small derby hat, but what was even more fascinating was the fact that the figure walked about two inches above the floor! After the figure had disappeared, David thought it was all his imagination. A particularly bright eight-year-old, he was not easily taken in by fantasies or daydreams.

But the strange figure reappeared several times, and eventually David came to the conclusion that it was real. He asked his parents whether he could swap rooms with them and they agreed to let his sleep downstairs. It was about that time that his mother told him that she had heard the old piano playing at night downstairs. She had thought that it was the cat climbing up on the keys, but one night the piano played in plain view of herself and one of her daughters, without even a trace of the cat in the room. There was also the sound of pages in a book being turned in the same area, although nobody had a book or turned any pages.

David settled down in his room on the lower floor and finally forgot all about his ghostly experiences. Shortly after, he heard a crunching noise on the stairs, as if someone were walking on them. He assumed it was his mother coming down the stairs to tell him to turn off his radio, but no one came.

As he grew older, he moved back upstairs, since the room on the ground floor had become too small for him. This proved to be somewhat of a strain for him: many times he would be lying in bed when someone would call his name. But there never was anyone there. Exasperated, the youngster spoke up, challenging the ghost to give some sign of his presence so that there could be communication between them. "If you can hear me, make a noise," David said to his ghost. At that very moment, the door to his room began to rattle without apparent cause.

Still unconvinced, since the door had rattled before because of natural causes, David continued his monologue with, "If you are there, show yourself," and at that moment he heard a strange noise behind him. The door to his closet, which had been closed, was slowly opening. This wasn't very reassuring, even though it might have represented some kind of dialogue with the ghost.

Shortly thereafter, and in broad daylight, just as he had gotten home from school, David heard a very loud noise in the upper portion of the house, as if all their cats were tearing each other to pieces and a lot of coat hangers were falling down. Quickly, David ran up the stairs—only to find neither cats nor fallen coat hangers. And to this day, David doesn't know who the strange visitor was.

• • •

Lana T. is one of seven children from eastern Missouri who has ESP to a considerable extent. Three of her sisters also have this ability. Today she is a housewife, and she and her husband live in a big city in central Missouri. Clairvoyant dreams and other verified incidents of ESP led to an interest in the much-maligned Ouija board, and she and her three sisters, Jean, Judy, and Tony, became veritable addicts of this little gadget. A close friend and her husband moved into a nearby house in the same community, without realizing that the house had become available due to the suicide of the previous owner.

Mrs. T.'s friend had come from another state, so the local facts were not too well known to her. When the new owner discovered that her neighbor, Lana T., had psychic gifts and an interest in occult matters, she confided freely in her. It appeared that one of the bathrooms was always cold, regardless of the weather outside or the temperature in the rest of the house; a certain closet door would simply not stay closed; and the heat register was bound to rattle of its own volition. Objects would move from one place to another, without anyone having touched them. Footsteps were heard in the hall, as if someone were pacing up and down. Once the new owner saw a whitish mist which dissolved immediately when she spoke to it.

Her husband, the publisher of a local newspaper, would not even discuss the matter, considering it foolish. But one night he woke up and informed her that he had just been touched by a cold, clammy hand.

This was enough to convince the new owner to consult with her neighbor. Lana T. offered to try and find out who the disturbing ghost was. Together with one of her sisters, she sat down with her trusty Ouija board, and asked it to identify the disturbing entity in the house. Ouija board communication is slow and sometimes boring, but, in this instance, the instrument rapidly identified the communicator as a certain Ted. A chill went down Mrs. T.'s spine, for Ted was the man who had committed suicide in her friend's house.

From then on, a veritable conversation ensued between Mrs. T. and the ghost, in which he explained that he was angry because the new owner had burned something of his. Mrs. T. asked what the new owner could do to satisfy him, and the angry ghost replied that she should destroy something of her own to make up for his loss—something white. When Mrs. T. described her conversation with the ghost to the new owner of the house, the lady was mystified. She could not recall having burned anything belonging to the former owner. Back to the Ouija board went Mrs. T. When she demanded that the ghost describe the item in question more fully, he replied, somewhat impatiently, that it had been white with green trim and had the letters SFCC on it. Mrs. T. returned to her neighbor with this additional information. This time she struck paydirt: shortly after the couple from out of state had moved into the house, the lady of the house had discovered an old golf cap in the top drawer of one of her closets, white with green trim and the initials of the country club, SFCC, on it! The cap had somehow bothered her, so she had tossed it into the trash can and the contents of the can were later burned. The ghost had told the truth. But how could she satisfy his strange whim in return? At this time she and her husband had considered buying a small, expensive white marble statue. They decided to forego this pleasure. Perhaps their sacrifice of this "white" item would make up for the lost golf cap? Evidently it did—for the house has been quiet ever since!

• • •

Mrs. Edith F. is the wife of a law enforcement officer in the west. Her husband puts very little credence in anything "supernatural," but Mrs. F. knows otherwise. The house she and her family live in is only about twelve years old, and fifteen years before, the area was still "in the country," although people may have lived there in a previous house. In fact, rumor has it that some old houses were torn down on the land where her house now stands. In the summer of 1972, a series of odd incidents began which convinced Mrs. F. of the reality of another dimension.

At the time her nine-year-old son was in the basement family room, watching television. On the north wall of this large room there was a door leading to a storeroom. A rollaway bed had been put there for possible summer company, and the boy was on this particular bed, propped up with a large pillow. He had just finished a snack, and was about to brush the crumbs from under him, when he happened to look up and saw an old woman standing beside the bed, staring at him. He looked away from her for a moment, then returned his eyes to her; she was still there. Frightened, he began to yell for his mother, at which the woman moved back towards the door. The door opened about two inches, and she quickly slid through it, as if she were two-dimensional.

By that time Mrs. F. arrived downstairs and found her son so frightened he could hardly talk. He described the visitor as very old, with black and gray hair parted in the middle, wearing a long black dress and a single pair of colored beads. Mrs. F. decided not to discuss it with her husband, who would only scoff at it, but to return to the basement with her twenty-year-old daughter to see whether anything would occur in their presence. The two women stood on the spot where the boy had seen the ghost and asked her what she wanted of them. For a moment, nothing happened. Then, suddenly, Mrs. F. felt as though someone were lifting her right arm which turned tingly and raised up in front of her by its own volition! She broke out in goose pimples and quickly whirled around, running back upstairs.

For several days, she did not dare go back to the basement out of fear that the phenomenon might repeat itself. But on the fourth day, Mrs. F. could not hold back any longer; she had to know what the ghost wanted. Somehow she felt she would get it by writing. Again she went to the basement with her twenty-year-old daughter, said a prayer for protection from evil, and stood upright with a pen in her right hand—why, she didn't really know, for she is *left*-handed. She asked aloud if there was anyone present, and the pen wrote, "Yes. You must watch out for woman," and then it drew an arrow toward the northern part of the room. Mrs. F. demanded to know what the ghost wanted, and in reply, the pencil in her hand wrote, "Priest. Hear my confession." Mrs. F. demanded to know what her name was, and the ghost identified herself as Mary Arthur.

With this information Mrs. F. went to the Reverend L.B., a Methodist minister, whom, she hoped, would have an open mind concerning occult phenomena. He decided to accompany the two women back to the house. He, too, stood in the basement and asked the ghost to give him a sign that she was present. A lamp, which they knew to be in good order, blinked on and off several times in response to their questions. Then, again through automatic writing, the ghost informed them that she had died at age eighty-nine, had had nine children, and knew she had passed on in 1959. Confession was needed to release her to the next level of existence, but the Methodist minister could not help her, she explained; it had to be a Catholic priest. The Reverend B. offered to talk to his Catholic colleague, but Mrs. F. suggested the ghost might find peace in nearby St. Agnes Church. On this note, the presence disappeared and was gone until the following Monday.

On that day, Mrs. F. was in the basement room, working on an ironing board. It was a very warm day, but suddenly she was startled by walking into a blast of icy air on the spot where the ghost had been originally observed by her son. Quickly she called for her daughter to join her and watch. After a moment, her daughter complained that her arm was being lifted the way her mother's had been before. She felt as if someone held it, and the arm felt tingly. Mrs. F. grabbed a pencil and paper from a nearby desk and gave it to her daughter. Her daughter then wrote "Mary" in exactly the same handwriting as Mrs. F. had originally. Then she handed the pencil and paper back to her mother, afraid to continue. So the mother continued the communication and the ghost wrote "Mary Arthur." Gradually, the reasons for her presence became clear. "Father, forgive me, for I have sinned," the ghost wrote, and demanded that the note be taken to a Roman Catholic priest. But Mrs. F. instead suggested that Mary call out to her loved ones to take her away from the place so she could find peace. "No, because of my sins," the ghost replied, and when Mrs. F. wanted to know what the sins consisted of, she simply said, "the marriage."

It was then that Mrs. F. learned that Mary had been born Catholic, had left the church and married a Lutheran and had had nine children with him. To her, this marriage was illegal, sinful. Eventually, the Roman Catholic clergy got into the act, but a special priest would have to be sent to exorcise Mary's sins. This did not sit well with Mrs. F., nor with her Methodist friend, neither of whom thought that Mary was evil.

Time passed, and things seemed to quiet down in the basement. Then, on Labor Day of the same year, 1972, with her husband and son fast asleep in bed, Mrs. F. was in the kitchen canning tomatoes from their garden. Again she felt Mary's presence upstairs, a strange feeling that was hard to describe. Again, her right arm was tingling and her fingers felt as they did when

Mary first wanted to write something through her. However, since the Roman Catholic clergy had been reluctant to enter the case, Mrs. F. determined to ignore her promptings. Here she was, washing tomatoes at her kitchen sink, when all of a sudden she heard a *plop!* behind her, turned around, and saw one of the tomatoes lying split open in the middle of the floor. Since she was the only person in the kitchen, there was no rational explanation for the fall of the tomato. Had it merely fallen off the counter, it would have gone straight down instead of jumping four feet away!

Quietly, Mrs. F. turned in the direction where she assumed her ghost lady was and reprimanded her for throwing the tomato. "They are saying special prayers at the church for you," she said, and asked Mary to go there and wait for her delivery.

Everything was quiet after that. About ten days later, a lamp in Mrs. F.'s living room blinked on and off four times as if the ghost were trying to tell her she was leaving. This time Mrs. F. did not feel the tingling sensation in her arm, and somehow felt that this was a farewell message. And since that time there has been no sign of Mary's presence. With the help of her minister friend, Mrs. F. was able to check the records of various funeral homes in the area. A Mary Arthur was buried in 1959.

• • •

Mrs. E. never had any interest in the occult nor experiences along ghostly lines until after her father died. It was a great loss to her and the family, since he had been a pillar of strength and had handled all their affairs. Shortly after he died, Mrs. E. was sitting in her mother's house and suddenly, without explanation, she found herself picking up a pen. On the back of a used envelope she wrote the words, "Tell Mama to take that will to the lawyer." Her mother had added some postscripts to her father's will, but had not realized that these requests would not be honored unless and until they had been witnessed and notarized again by an attorney!

• • •

Jananne B. is an attractive twenty-five-year-old girl, who has had experiences with the unseen since she was very small. While she was visiting her aunt in New Jersey, she remembers clearly seeing a figure in the old carriage house. There was no one in the carriage house at the time. At age seventeen, Jananne was spending a weekend with another aunt, also in New Jersey. Both women were occupying the same bed. In the middle of the night the young girl sat up in bed, waking her aunt. There was a tall man in a brown suit standing next to the bed, she explained, and went on to describe his brown hair and handlebar mustache in great detail. Without saying a word, her aunt got up and brought out the family album. Leafing through it, Jananne pointed at one particular picture: it was her great-grandfather. She had never seen pictures of him, nor, of course, ever met him. He had died in the very room and bed in which the two women were sleeping at the time.

When she was twenty-four years old, Jananne moved into what was formerly her brother's room, her brother having moved to his own apartment. The very first night she stayed in the room, she felt a presence, and couldn't sleep. Somehow the room had always been the stuffiest room in the house but that night it was particularly cold. This upset her greatly since she had put in a great deal of time and effort to redecorate it to her taste. Somehow she went to sleep that night, trying to forget or ignore her feelings. A few nights later she woke up in the middle of the night, feeling extremely cold. As she sat up in bed, she saw a woman out of the corner of her eye. The woman seemed middle-aged, with brown hair pulled back in a very plain bun, wearing a long, straight skirt and a white, ruffled blouse with long sleeves and high collar.

Jananne did not experience a feeling of fear, for somehow she knew the spirit was friendly. The next morning, just as she was about to wake up, she saw the name "Elly" being written on the wall above her shelves. There were other lines around the name, but before she could make them out, the vision faded. Since she keeps a dream log, recording all unusual dreams, she immediately wrote this incident down before she could forget it. She also told her mother about the incidents. Time passed, and several months later a local psychic came to the house to do a reading for the family, using her bedroom to work in.

The psychic described the entity in the room precisely the way Jananne had seen it. By now Jananne was not the only one to be aware of the ghost. Various friends also heard footsteps overhead while sitting in a room directly underneath hers, and had seen the lights dim of their own volition. Because of the ghostly presence, Jananne's room is unusually cold, and she would frequently complain about it. Not long ago, when she remarked how cold it was, the door to the outdoor widow's walk flew wide open and her bedroom door shut of its own volition.

This happened a number of times, making the room even colder. On several occasions, Jananne came home to find her bedroom door tightly shut, and very hard to open. Once inside, she noticed that her bedspread was on the floor, propped up against the door from the inside. No one could have placed it there except from inside the room—and the room had been locked.

Soon enough Jananne realized that she had to get used to sharing her room with the strange lady. Once her mind was made up to accept her as a companion, the phenomenon became less annoying. A short time ago she decided to take some random pictures of the room, to see whether anything unusual would show up on them. Only the available room light was used, no flash light or electrical lighting. Two of the pictures came back from the laboratory with a white mist on them, one of them showing the name "Elly" indistinctly, but nevertheless apparent beyond the shadow of a doubt. Jananne showed the photographs to her brother, a professional photographer, and to some of his friends. They agreed that double exposure or light leaks were out; the white mist appears to be blotchy, almost like smoke, whereas light leaks would tend to be uniform.

Jananne realizes that Elly is able to manifest for her only because she is psychic. If she needed any further proof of her ability in this respect, it was furnished to her a month later when a friend took her to a certain lady's trailer home for dinner. Jananne's friend asked her to dress lightly because it was always warm there, he said.

But when they arrived at the trailer, it was unusually cold inside. They were having a quiet conversation after dinner, sitting on the couch, when Jananne looked up and saw the figure of a very sad young man standing in the entrance to the hallway. His head was bowed, and he seemed very lost. Since the hostess had turned out to be rather on the nervous side, Jananne decided not to tell her about the apparition. But on the way home, she informed her friend what she had seen, describing the man in detail. Her friend swallowed hard, then informed her that the husband of their hostess had disappeared shortly after returning from Vietnam. Three months later his body was found in the woods; he had committed suicide.

. . .

Dorothy Mark-Moore was twelve years old when her Aunt Mary bought a house in Green Brook, New Jersey. The house was on Washington Street and the year was 1933. All the members of the family had retired for the night, and it was a rather warm night at that, so Dorothy thought she'd roll up her pajama legs, and go to sleep like that. She awoke with a start in the early hours of the morning and looked around the room. It so happened that it was a moonlit night so she could clearly make out the objects in the room.

As she looked toward the window, she saw a woman walk in, return to the window, look out it and then turn toward her. Frightened, Dorothy pretended to be asleep for a moment, but then she opened her eyes again and to her amazement saw a nun standing there, looking at her from head to foot. Then the nun came over and moved her hand onto her legs. But when the nun touched Dorothy's legs, it felt "like an old dried-out piece of wood."

The ghostly nun was now close enough to the bed for Dorothy to make out a ring on her hand and beads around her waist, with a large cross dangling at the end of it. The woman appeared to be in her thirties, and seemed quite solid. Suddenly Dorothy realized she was looking at a ghost. She shot up and looked straight into the nun's face. For a moment, girl and ghost stared at each other. Then the nun's face softened as she walked away from Dorothy and vanished into the wall.

Four years later the ghostly nun returned. This time Dorothy was asleep in another bedroom of the same house and it was around seven o'clock in the morning. All of a sudden, Dorothy heard loud organ music and sat up in bed to find out where it came from. The music became so loud she could not stand it and fell back onto the pillows. It felt as if an invisible hand were holding her down. At that moment, the nun entered the room with a gentleman in his forties, with dark hair and brown eyes, wearing a dark blue serge suit. Dorothy was petrified, especially as the organ music increased to an almost ear-splitting level. Looking at the two apparitions, she noticed that they were reciting the Lord's Prayer, from the movement of their lips. As they did so, the music became less loud, and the two figures slowly walked towards the door. As they left the room, the music stopped abruptly. At that moment, Dorothy seemed to snap out of her trance state, sat up in bed, and quickly grabbed all her clothes, running to the bathroom and locking herself in. When she had regained her composure, she made some inquiries about the house and learned that a gentleman of that description had killed himself some fifty years before in the very bathroom into which she had locked herself.

• • •

It was a warm weekend in June of 1971, and a group of New Jersey college students decided to throw a party at a place known as "The Farmhouse," which had been rented for the occasion. Most of the young people were between nineteen and twenty-two years of age, and, as the party progressed, the spirits were high.

Sometime that evening, a boy named Arthur D., son of a police-man, crashed the party and a fight ensued. According to local newspapers, the fight was part of the shindig, but according to others, the boy was ejected and lay in wait to get even with those who had turned him down. As a result of the fighting, Arthur lay dead in the street, due to wounds received from a knife. Glen F., a twenty-two-year-old youth at the party, was arrested for his mur-der. Another boy was in the local hospital, seriously injured, but expected to survive. . . . That was in June, 1971, and it was one graduation party long remembered in the area.

In the summer of 1972 the house was rented out to a certain Mrs. Gloria Brown. Mrs. Brown and three children were sleeping in the hayloft of the barn, which is located a certain distance from the main house. One of the girls saw a light in the house go on downstairs and the figure of a man which she thought was her father. When she investigated, the man tried to grab her. She screamed and her brothers came to her aid. By that time the "man" had run away. Later that summer, a friend was staying with the Browns one evening. There was a knock at the door of the main house about two o'clock in the morning. The friend got up and answered it, but there was no one outside. She went back to bed, only to be awakened again. This time she opened the door and looked through the screen door to see whether there might be someone outside.

There was a man standing outside all right, and she asked whether he was hurt or needed help. Then she noticed that he had neither face nor hands, and was only a whitish, swirly sub-stance! Horror-stricken, she stared at him as he disappeared just as suddenly as he had come.

At this writing, the restless boy is still unable to find peace. For him, the unlucky party has never broken up.

• • •

Yellow Frame Church is an old country church at Yellow Frame, New Jersey. It stands in one of the most isolated areas of the state and is but little-known to people outside the immediate area. Even today there is only the minister's house and a grave-yard across the street, but no other dwellings close by. In the early 1800s a new minister came to Yellow Frame and, after his very first sermon, dropped dead. He was duly buried in the churchyard across from the church. For unknown reasons, his body was taken some years later from the churchyard and moved to another cemetery at Johnsonburg, two miles down the road.

So much for the background of the old building. I wouldn't be writing about it if it weren't for a recent report from an alert reader, Mrs. Johanna C., who lives in a nearby town. Apparently there had been an incident involving a woman on her way home early in the morning, while it was still dark, not long ago. When the lady passed the church she heard choir music coming from it and saw that both doors were wide open. Curious as to who might be playing the organ that early in the morning, or, rather, that late at night, she stepped up and peered into the church: the inside of the building was quite dark, and when she stepped inside she noticed that there was no one in the church. Frightened, she left in a hurry.

In the late 1960s, Mr. C. and a group of friends, who had heard the account of the organ music, decided to see for themselves whether there was anything unusual about the church. As so many others who think that Halloween is the time to look for ghosts, Mr. C. and friends picked the night of October 31 to do their ghost hunt. Of course, there is no connection between Halloween, the solemn holiday of witchcraft, the Old Religion, and ghosts; but popular superstition will always link them, since ghosts and witches *seem* to belong to the same level of reference. At any rate, Mr. C. and his friends arrived at Yellow Frame Church at exactly midnight and bravely walked up the steps of the church. At that hour, the church was, of course, closed. As they confronted the locked doors, the doors suddenly swung open of their own volition, startling the visitors. But this did not stop them; they stepped inside the church and, as they did so, each one of the group noticed a strange pressure on his ears as if the air were pushing against them!

One in the group called out, "Reverend, oh Reverend!" but there was no answer. The eerie stillness of the building was too much for them, and they left in a hurry.

A year later, again on Halloween, Mrs. C. went along with the same group to see whether she could experience anything out of the ordinary. They arrived at the church shortly before midnight, driving by it at first to get a look at it. They noticed that both doors were shut. A few minutes later they returned to see that one of the doors was slightly open. They parked their car and stepped inside the church. At that moment Mrs. C. could also feel the strange pressure on her ears. She also felt as if someone were hiding in the church, watching them. There was a peaceful feeling about it, almost, she explained, as if she were being wrapped in a blanket. Mrs. C. decided to spend some time inside the church to see whether it was truly haunted, but the men would have no part of it and insisted that they all leave again. As they were discussing whether or not they should go immediately, they clearly heard what appeared to be footsteps in the leaves. It sounded as if someone were walking around just outside the building. However, they did not stay around long enough to find out whether there was, in fact, someone walking who was not a member of their group.

But the matter did not give Mrs. C. any rest, so she returned to the church once more in the company of a girl friend, this time during daylight hours. She managed to meet the present minister's wife, telling her of their experiences. To their relief, the minister's wife was not at all shocked, and mentioned that not long ago, she had awakened at six in the morning, and, peering out the window toward the church, became aware of lights in the church going on and off as if someone were signaling with them. There is also a tradition in the area that the church is haunted by the restless spirit of the original minister, who doesn't like being buried in the wrong cemetery and comes up the Yellow Frame Road searching for his original resting place.

. . .

ESSAY

from The Law of the Ghost

BY

SIR ARTHUR CONAN DOYLE

It is safe to say that for some centuries to come the human race will be very actively engaged in defining the laws which regulate psychic affairs, and it is fortunately a line of study which has the peculiar advantage to those who indulge in it that they can pursue it just as well, and probably better, from the other side of the veil. At present there is work lying to hand for a hundred investigators. The innumerable records which exist in various forms, and which are scattered throughout papers, magazines, reports of learned societies, family traditions, etc., are like masses of ore which have been extracted from the ground but are still lying in dumps waiting to be separated into precious ingots on the one side and slag-heap on the other. They have to be examined, collected into classes, reviewed in the light of our ever-increasing psychic knowledge, and an endeavor made to find underlying principles running through this vague collection of matter, so that at last we may touch solid ground by getting hold of some elementary laws. The first thing is that we should have authentic cases so that the foundation of our reasoning may be sound. The second is to compare these authentic cases together and see what common characteristics they possess, shirking nothing and following the facts wherever they lead without any preliminary prejudice. This is, of course, the true scientific fashion, but it is unfortunately one which has been neglected by most scientific men in approaching this new subject which would not fit in with their preconceived ideas. Let us hunt among these fascinating problems for shards and splinters out of which a noble mosaic will one day be constructed, and let us see whether here and there we may not find two or three pieces which fit together, and give some idea of a permanent pattern, even though it be a fantastic one. I will begin by telling three stories which seem to be absolutely authentic, and then we shall endeavor to trace some underlying connection. . . .

In July, 1807, a Mrs. Goddard was buried [in a vault], and her [wooden] coffin was found undisturbed in February, 1808, when a child named Mary Chase was laid in a leaden casket beside her. For four years the vault was closed, but in July, 1812, it was opened to admit a Miss Dorcas Chase. The horrified workmen found the coffin of the infant standing on its head in a corner. It was supposed that some mischievous and sacrilegious wretch had been guilty of a senseless outrage, so after the coffin was rearranged the great marble slab was once again placed in position, to be opened next month when a Mr. Chase joined the family group within. During the month there seems to have been no disturbance.

In September, 1816, four years having again elapsed, the vault was opened once more to admit an infant, Samuel Arnes. Once again all was in horrible confusion, and the coffins littered across one another. The affair was now becoming a scandal and the talk of the whole settlement. . . .

Three years later, on July 7th, 1819, Miss Clarke was to be buried in the vault. So great was the public excitement that the governor, Lord Combermere, of Peninsula fame, attended the ceremony with his staff and aides-de-camp. Things were as bad as ever. The wooden coffin was intact, but the others were scattered in all directions. Lord Combermere was so interested that he had the whole structure searched and sounded, but there was no hidden approach or underground passage. It was an insoluble mystery. The coffins were rearranged and the floor carefully sanded so that footsteps would be revealed. The door was cemented up, which seems to have been done on each occasion, but this time the Governor affixed his own particular seal. The British Government had officially entered the lists against the powers of darkness.

It is humiliating to add that the powers of darkness seemed not in the least abashed either by the Governor or by the Empire which he represented. Next year, in April, 1820, it was determined that an official inspection should be made without waiting for a fresh interment. . . . The cement was then broken and the slab removed. . . . On exposing the interior it was found to the horror and amazement of the party that the difficulty in opening the vault had been caused by the fact that a leaden coffin within, so heavy that several men could hardly move it, had been jammed upside down against the slab. There was great confusion within but no marks upon the sand which covered the floor. So horrified was everyone by this final test that the bodies were now removed and buried elsewhere. The empty vault remains, and is likely for many centuries to remain. . . .

. . . [To] see if any other such cases may fall into line with this one, we have not far to seek, for one is quoted in . . . the *European Magazine* for September, 1815, under the heading "The Curious vault at Stanton in Suffolk." In the magazine account it says:

> On opening the vault some years since, several leaden coffins with wooden cases that had been fixed on biers, were found displaced to the great astonishment of many. The coffins were placed as before, when some time ago, another of the family dying, they were a second time found displaced. Two years after they were found not only all off the biers, but one coffin as heavy as to require eight men to raise it was found on the fourth step that leads into the vault.

The next case. . . . comes from the Livonian village of Ahrensburg in the Baltic, and remote as the scene is, the evidence is well attested.

There is a considerable cemetery in the village, which is dotted with small private chapels, each of them with a family burial vault beneath it. The finest of these belonged to a family named Buxhoewden. . . . [In] the early summer of the year 1844, . . . a member of the Buxhoewden family died, and the hearse horses on approaching the cemetery showed . . . signs of terror. . . . The service in the chapel was interrupted by hollow groans, which may have been imagined by a congregation who were already predisposed to alarm. What was not imagination, however, was the fact that those who afterwards descended into the vault found the coffins there, which had been in rows, cast into a confused heap upon the wooden floor. These coffins seem to have been of massive oak, very strongly and heavily made. This might have been the work of some enemy to the family, but the doors of the vault had been secured and the locks were intact. There was always the possibility of false keys, however, so the coffins were replaced in their order, and the place very carefully secured.

As the agitation of the horses and the general unrest of the community still continued the chief man of the district, Baron de Guldenstubbe, took up the matter officially. . . . With two of his family he made a preliminary examination, and then finding the coffins once again in confusion, he formed a committee of investigation consisting of himself, the local bishop, the Bürgermeister, a physician named Luce and four representative citizens.

On entering the vault they again found that the enemy had been at work and that the contents were scattered in all directions. Only three coffins, those of a very saintly grandmother and of two little children, were undisturbed. . . .

Everything was now closed up once more and the disconsolate committee withdrew, after placing heavy seals upon the door. Before leaving the vault fine ashes were scattered all over the wooden floor, and also over the steps leading down, and the pavement of the chapel. Finally guards were set for three days and nights. It must be admitted that they did things thoroughly in the village of Ahrensburg. At the end of that time the Commission returned in full state with the whole population lining the churchyard rails, eager to hear the result.

The seals were unbroken, the door unopened, but the interior of the vault was in the usual state of chaos. No sign at any point was found upon the ashes and no human feet had entered, but great forces had none the less been at work. The secret powers, reinforced rather than abashed by the recent visit of the Commission, had wrought far greater mischief than before. All the coffins were scattered, save the same three which had been exempt before. Some of the heaviest had been placed upside-down so that the corpse was on its head, and in one instance the lid had burst and the right arm of the inmate, who was a man who had died by his own hand, was protruding and pointing towards the ceiling. Such was the fearsome spectacle which greeted the Commission. . . .

The result of these gruesome phenomena was that the coffins were removed from the vault and were buried in earth, after which complete tranquillity seems to have descended upon the little village. . . .

No doubt many other such cases could be recorded, but here at least are three which appear to be authentic and which reproduce the same characteristics. If relics of some strange animal were found in three different localities, the first conclusion among men of science would be that such an animal did exist, and was henceforth to be included among the creatures of earth. The next proceeding would be to compare the relics and to endeavor to reconstruct some image of the newcomer. In the same way these three cases may be said to fairly establish the fact of these curious phenomena. . . . When we compare the cases, however, and to deduce the underlying laws, the psychic student can at best only point to a few possible indications which may be of value.

 . . . [O]ne or more living people in a confined space which is afterwards closed up may leave behind them something human and yet invisible, which is sufficiently subtle to be used by forces from the other side as a basis for material phenomena. All movements of solid objects, touched or untouched, in the presence of a medium are to be explained in this fashion, and the force may be expected to be stronger when confined within a limited space. In the case of the Cheriton dug-out, which occupied public attention a couple of years ago, the worker and the boy were busy in a narrow excavation. One or other was mediumistic— that is to say, emitted to an unusual extent this emanation—with the result that the phenomena occurred in the same way, though with less force, when both of them had left the work for their luncheon, as Mr. Jaques, the owner of the property, was able to testify. Let us suppose that in the case of each of these three vaults there was an accumulation of this mysterious, but very certain, power left behind by the coffin-bearers, and possibly reinforced by the committees of inquiry, who would have been very amazed had they been told that they were, in all probability, themselves contributing to the phenomena. There, I think, you have the physical basis which is necessary for every spirit manifestation, for it cannot too often or too clearly be insisted upon that spirits are not omnipotent and irresponsible forces, but that they are under a rule of law no less strict than our own. One of these laws is that a physical basis is needed for every physical manifestation. . . . No ghost was ever self-supporting. He can exist without our help, but he cannot manifest to human eyes without drawing his material from human (or possibly animal) sources. That, as it seems to me, is one of the basic laws of the new world of science.

There is some evidence, which could be cited in full if it did not lead us down a lengthy side street, that when a life has been cut short before it has reached its God-appointed term, whether the cause be murder or suicide (of accident I speak with less confidence), there remains a store of unused vitality which may, where the circumstances are favorable, work itself off in capricious and irregular ways. This is, I admit, a provisional theory, but it has been forced upon my mind by many considerations. Such a theory would go some way to explain, or at least to throw some dim light upon, the disturbances which from all past time have been associated with scenes of violence and murder. If it could be conceived that the unseen part of a man is divisible into the higher, which passes on as spirit, and the lower which represents animal functions and mere unused vitality, then it is this latter which has not been normally worked off in a life prematurely ended, and which may express itself in strange semi-intelligent fashion afterwards. In dreams one is conscious of some such division, where the higher functions occasionally bring us back touches of the most spiritual; while the lower functions, deprived for the time of judgment, humor and all the spirit qualities, evolve a capricious and grotesque life of their own, which has neither reason nor sense of proportion and yet seems very real to us in our slumbers. It is not a subject upon which one could be dogmatic, but the days are passing when all such cases can be disposed of by being brushed aside and ignored as senseless superstition. Some sort of framework must be formed into which they can be fitted, and with fuller knowledge the fit will be closer. . . .

One remark should be made before passing on to another form of ghostly manifestation. It has been said that the basis for physical results lies in the human organism. It is not meant, however, that there is any relation between the small amount often taken from the medium and the great physical results obtained. It is clear that the unseen forces can get great power from a limited supply of this subtle material. In the case carefully observed and noted by Professor Zöllner of Leipzig, a beam of wood which two horses could not have dragged apart was shattered into pieces in the presence of [a witness]. A friend of mine who was present at a meeting of the Goligher circle saw a table ascend in the air and remain there, although four strong men did all they could to drag it down. It is true that in a sitting of this sort the medium, Miss Goligher, frequently registered a loss of weight amounting to a stone in a séance upon the weighing-dial which Dr. Crawford had erected, but it is clear that the force exerted by the unseen powers was very much greater than this and was due to their own manipulation of the material which her organism had provided. In some of the sittings of D. D. Home, the force was so great that the whole building used to shake as if a heavy train were passing below it.

And here comes one of the mysteries which bear directly upon that definition of spirit law which is so desirable. In spite of the possibility of using vast power there is a clear, and so far as credible records go, an unbroken ordinance that a ghost may not for its own personal ends destroy anything or injure anyone. This may seem in contradiction to the broken coffins, but that may not have been for personal ends, but an accident due to the falling about of the heavy weights. Here is an authentic case in illustration:

A great friend of mine, a Roman Catholic priest, whose word could not be doubted by anyone who knew him, was sent for a rest cure to a lonely house upon the coast which was frequently used by other priests for the same purpose. Save for an old crone and one or two charitable visitors, he was absolutely alone. After a few days he became less conscious of strange noises in the house, which at last reached such a point that, to quote his own description, "it sounded at night as if there were a steam-engine snorting and clanking in the room below." Nothing was visible, but the sounds were incessant and were heard by two visitors as clearly as by the inmate. The priest is himself open more than most men to psychic impressions, and upon that night he had a dream or vision which was so absolutely clear that he determined to act upon it. He descended in the morning and asked the old woman whether there was not an unused room in the basement. She answered that there was. He entered it and found that he had already seen it in his dream—a small dusty, cobwebbed place with some old books of theology heaped in the corners. He walked at once to one of these heaps, picked up a book as in his dream, opened it, took out a sheet of written paper, glanced at it to make sure that it was really as revealed and then carried it into the kitchen, where he stuffed it between the bars of the grate. The paper was a written preparation for confession, made out by some overconscientious or over-methodical inmate of the house, who had noted down a good many more things than were desirable for public perusal. Presumably he had died shortly afterwards and had been worried by the recollection of this

document, which he then took these means to have destroyed.
There were no further disturbances of any sort within the house.

Now here is a story which is undoubtedly true and which cannot be met by any of the ingenious explanations of the honest
but skeptical Researcher. If the subconscious knowledge of my
friend could have told him that the paper was there, it certainly
could not have caused the noises which alarmed him. It has to be
examined as a fact, as the zoologist already quoted would exam-
ine the skin of his rare animal. The unhappy spirit could
apparently draw power either from the old housekeeper or, as is
more likely, from the young and psychic priest, to shake the very
house with vibrations, and yet with all this power he could not
destroy a frail sheet of paper, but had to bring its destruction
about in this indirect fashion. This seems to be a solid and note-
worthy conclusion. All authentic tales where spirits linger,
earth-bound because they appear to be worried over earthly
things, concealed treasure, lost documents, or other such matters, come into this category, and the question which one
naturally asks, "Why can't they set the matter right for themselves?" is answered by, "They have not the power. It is against
the law."

I believe that all these varied experiences have been sent to us
not to amuse us by tales to be told and then forgotten but as the
essential warp and woof of a new spiritual garment which is to be
woven for the modern world. We live in an age which has long
demanded a sign, yet when the sign was sent it was blind to it. I
cannot understand the frame of mind of those who view proofs
of survival which appear in the Bible as of most vital importance,
and yet close their mind to the same thing when they reappear
before our very eyes. I believe most of the evidence in the sacred
books, where it is not perverted by mistranslation, interposition
or forgery, to be perfectly good evidence, but no honest mind
could say that judged by human standards of credibility it could,
for an instant, compare in its demonstration of the fate which

awaits the soul, with the psychic revelations of recent years. In the latter case the witnesses are thousands in number, are men of the highest credibility, and have placed in many cases their personal experiences upon record so that any objection can be lodged. Modern Britain does not disprove but confirms ancient Judea. We are in a more scientific age, however, and we wish to know the how and the why. Such inquiries are no longer, with so great a wealth of material, beyond the scope of our brains. In this article I have endeavored to indicate two well-marked laws: the one that it is the effluvia of the human organism which furnish the basis of physical manifestations from the unseen; the other, that there is a strict limitation of psychic power which does not prevent noise and subsequent disturbance, but does stand in the way of destruction or personal violence.

Sir Arthur Conan Doyle (1859–1930) was a British writer, playwright, and spiritualist. His best-known creation, the legendary detective Sherlock Holmes, first appeared in *A Study in Scarlet* (1887), and later in mysteries including *The Valley of Fear* and *The Hound of the Baskervilles*. A longstanding member of the Society for Psychical Research, Conan Doyle also was known for his experiences with mediums and psychic phenomena, some of which he recorded in *The Edge of the Unknown*, from which this essay is reprinted.